Introdu

CW01466449

This is an entirely new expand walks around Hereford, which Leominster. A few of the original walks have been used, but most are new ones, and they all reflect my own favourite parts of the countryside in this lovely county. The walks are all within easy reach of Hereford and/or Leominster, and all are accessible by public transport as well as by car. Bus services decrease all the time, but the ones used in this book are mainly major ones which should survive even the most draconian cuts. Bus timetables are on Herefordshire Council's website (www.herefordshire.gov.uk/public-transport).

The walks feature pastures, orchards and especially woods, hills and streams or rivers. Iron Age hill forts were usually built on hilltops, and many now have attractive woodland and/or good views, and several of the walks visit these evocative reminders of the past. Nature reserves are also usually in delightful settings, and the walks, especially those round Fownhope, take in several of these, including some belonging to the Herefordshire Wildlife Trust – an excellent organisation, always happy to welcome new members. The River Wye is one of the finest in Britain, and Hereford is the only city it goes through, so it will be no surprise to find that five of the walks in this book (3, 5, 7, 8 and 12) have a section along the Wye.

The walks use public rights of way, open access land or permissive paths; all of these can change with time, so please be tolerant and flexible and follow local instructions if routes have altered. I've walked all the routes in winter and summer and am indebted to the individuals and organisations, especially the Ramblers Association, who work hard to maintain paths and to keep them open.

Herefordshire is a county of great variety and beauty, as you'll soon discover if you're new to the area. It's also a largely unknown county, and on most of these walks you may not meet any other walkers, even in summer. Walks 14 and 19 are exceptions to this, but even there you'll be alone for most of the walks.

I am most grateful to Mike Thompson for allowing me to revise and update his original edition. My thanks are also due to Les Lumsdon, who has accompanied me on many walks around Herefordshire, and who has given me advice and encouragement.

Enjoy your walking!

EWYAS HAROLD COMMON & DULAS

DESCRIPTION This moderate 6½ mile walk goes through the attractive village of Ewyas Harold and up to its Common, a large open area which is rich in flowers and butterflies in summer. It continues through peaceful countryside with some good views from higher ground.

START Bus stop at Pontrilas shop and post office (a community shop and tea room, worth a visit), SO398276. If not visiting the shop, alight at Pontrilas telephone exchange stop about 200 yards further on (from Hereford).

DIRECTIONS The X3 bus between Hereford and Cardiff goes via Pontrilas. Parking is available on the road in Pontrilas, or you can make the walk two miles shorter by parking on the street in Ewyas Harold, in which case start at section 2

1 From the bus stop, if coming from Hereford, cross over and walk on, past the turning on the left to Monmouth, and over the river to the A465 main road. Cross this with great care and continue on a track opposite the turning. This goes over a bridge and round to the left through a gate. Soon leave the track by keeping LEFT of a fence, along a path and through a gate. The route now stays close to the Dulas brook on your left and crosses two fields separated by a stile. Go through a gate, pass a footbridge on the left, keeping ahead and round to the right, soon crossing a meadow to a stile half way along. Pass a house on the left and reach, via a stile, a drive taking you down to a road. Cross over and turn LEFT, soon keeping ahead to the village centre.

2 Just after the two pubs and the fish and chip shop (*and rare old black poplar immediately after it*), bear RIGHT past the post office and stores through a gate into the churchyard. Pass the church on your right to leave via another gate onto a quiet lane. Turn RIGHT. At the T junction at the end, turn LEFT. The road now takes you up to the Common over a cattle grid and past an information board. Soon fork RIGHT gently uphill. Turn LEFT by a bench on your right. When you reach a sign for The Prospect (a white house on the left), turn RIGHT over the grass close to the hedge on the left. Ignore a left turn but keep ahead round to the left and across the grass to a large gate ahead. Go through this into Ewyas Harold Meadows Reserve, owned by Butterfly Conservation (*information board just inside the gate*).

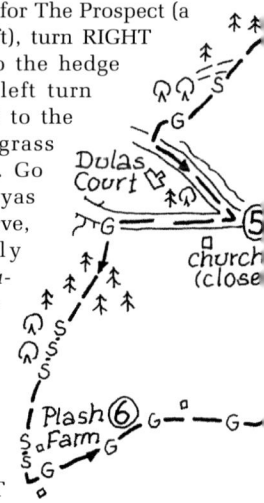

3 Turn RIGHT along the top of the meadow to pass through a gate. Now go diagonally LEFT down to a corner near a house. Bear RIGHT through a gate and straight up the bank and through another gate. Bear RIGHT across the meadow to leave the reserve via another gate/stile. Keep straight ahead up a wide grassy track, cross another track and at a T junction of tracks turn RIGHT. When you reach a water trough, turn LEFT to reach a track close to houses. Turn LEFT up this track. At a bench under trees, bear LEFT across the grass to reach a hedge; descend a short way next to this to cross a stile on your RIGHT.

4 Bear slightly RIGHT across the field to cross another stile by a gateway. Walk ahead towards farm buildings. Go through a gate between barns, then soon round to the LEFT, then to the RIGHT and over a stile ahead. Head slightly LEFT down the field towards trees and walk downhill by them, looking carefully for a rough path on your RIGHT leading to a stile. Cross this and follow the path downhill. Turn RIGHT at a T junction, then soon LEFT and LEFT again to emerge from the woodland over a stile. Bear RIGHT past a wall to leave the field via a gate/stile. Soon turn LEFT on a drive, in the grounds of Dulas Court care home. Soon pass

Cot Farm

Ewyas Harold Common

Ewyas Harold Meadows Reserve

The Prospect

Ewyas Harold Castle (remains)

N

0 ¼ mile

church

6 Now walk with the hedge on your left, through a gate, past a ruin and through another gate. When the hedge turns left, keep ahead across the grass, through a gap, across another field and through a gate. Ignore a waymarked gate on your right but quite soon turn RIGHT over a stile, then LEFT. Keep close to the hedge on your left to go through two gates with a field between them. Now keep RIGHT downhill to go through another gate. Walk past some old buildings. *The mound of former Ewyas Harold castle is now on your left. The owner has kindly provided a permissive route to the summit, where there is an excellent viewpoint. To get to this, follow the mound round to the left, go through a gate on the LEFT and soon another on the LEFT, then immediately turn LEFT up a very steep path (only for the sure-footed, can be very slippery). Return by the same route.* Bear LEFT, if you've just visited the summit, down the meadow to a kissing gate and go down steps to a gate leading to a road.

7 Turn RIGHT. Walk back through the village, Turn LEFT at the T-junction (signed to Hay-on-Wye), and just after the first house on the right, turn RIGHT along a drive and cross a stile. Now follow the route you came on

Dulas Brook

A465 to Hereford

START

Pontrilas

to Monmouth

A4651

a barn which has recently opened as a coffee shop, *currently only open on Mondays and Tuesdays*. Follow the drive round to the left and ahead to meet a road.

5 Turn RIGHT. Pass Dulas Church (*closed, but the churchyard is open and is renowned for its Spring flowers*). Soon, just before a bridge, turn LEFT through a gate and walk up the left hand side of the field. Cross a stile into woodland, then continue up over two more stiles to reach a field. Bear LEFT up the slope towards a farmhouse. Cross a stile ahead to the right of the house, and then head for the top right hand end of the field and cross another stile on your RIGHT. Turn LEFT, go through a gate and turn LEFT again. Walk past the house through the yard into a field via a gate.

earlier to walk close to the brook on your right back to Pontrilas.

WALK 2

KILPECK & SADDLEBOW

DESCRIPTION A moderate 7 mile (5½ if coming by car) walk, over farmland tracks and paths, through wooded dingles and along ancient hedgerows with constantly changing views of Herefordshire countryside. The walk involves some gradual ascents and descents, and some superb views; it also passes the church at Kilpeck, with its remarkable medieval carvings.

START Bus stop at Kilpeck Turn (the first turning to Kilpeck, coming on the A465 from Hereford), SO 439315. If coming by car, there is a small parking area next to Kilpeck Church, SO 445305; start the walk at section 2.

DIRECTIONS The X3 bus between Hereford and Cardiff stops at Kilpeck Turn. For car users, the route to the church is signed from Kilpeck Turn on the A465.

I Walk down the minor road towards Kilpeck. *The first turning on the left leads to St Devereux Church, much less visited than its famous neighbour, but worth a short detour, if only for its tranquil setting.* Cross the railway and a bridge over a stream. About 130 yards after the bridge, turn RIGHT through an easy-to-miss gap in the hedge, then turn half-left to walk uphill to a stile and gate leading to the churchyard. The church entrance is on the left. *Turn RIGHT immediately before the church if you want to visit the remains of Kilpeck Castle.* To continue the walk, pass the church and go through a gate to the car park.

2 Walk ahead along the road to the Kilpeck Inn. Turn RIGHT. When the road bends right, keep ahead (signed to the Village Hall). About 200 yards after the turning to 'Dippersmoor' on the right, turn RIGHT along a track next to a barn. Just after the barn bear half LEFT across a field. Go through trees with a fence on either side. Follow the track round to the RIGHT and then head for the far corner, which is now ahead of you to your left. Cross a stile/gate and walk along the

right hand edge of the field. 60 yards after the end of the wood, turn RIGHT through a gate into a meadow. Go down this to go through a gate in front of the rightmost house.

3 Turn LEFT. Soon go through a short stretch of woodland via stiles and two tiny footbridges (keep RIGHT twice after the first of these) to emerge in a meadow. Keep ahead across this, quite close to the hedge on the left, and leave over a stile. Turn LEFT and keep left. As the track finally levels off at a junction, turn half-LEFT through a gate, ignoring the entrance to a house to your left. Go through the next gate to walk along next to a fence. When you reach a stile on your right, bear LEFT, soon under a lone oak tree, to cross a stile in the hedge ahead. (Ignore another stile down on your left.)

4 Continue ahead via stiles through two fields and into a third. Here bear LEFT to cross a footbridge over a stream. Go slightly LEFT up the field to turn RIGHT over a stile by a gate. Keep ahead and, when you're level with a barn on your right, turn RIGHT through a gate, and immediately LEFT, staying close to the fence. Walk through the left hand side of a copse, re-entering the field through another gate. Stay on the right hand side of the field and leave it through a gate ahead. At once cross a stile into another field and aim diagonally left uphill to a gate near the corner. Once through this, walk up the left hand side of two fields via two gates to a road. Turn LEFT.

5 In several hundred yards, after passing a waymarked turning to 'Whitehouse' on the left, and soon after the line of telegraph wires leaves the road to the left, take the narrow path on the LEFT downhill through the bracken. *This path can become very overgrown in summer; if it's impassable, turn back along the road and follow section 6.* The downhill path widens and reaches a track. Turn LEFT, walk through a gate and turn RIGHT in front of a barn. Walk straight ahead down a green lane. Continue at section 7.

6 Ignore this section if you've managed to complete section 5. At the turning

(map)

to Hereford
A465
① START

St Devereux
⛪ Church

N

0 ——————— ¼
mile

Kilpeck
Church
Kilpeck
Castle
(remains)
② P
Kilpeck Inn
Kilpeck

Village
Hall

Dippersmoor
Wood

③

④

F.B.

Whitehouse

⑤

⑥

Saddlebow Hill
If this section is impassable return to point ⑥
⑦

⑧
Sizecroft

New
House
Farm

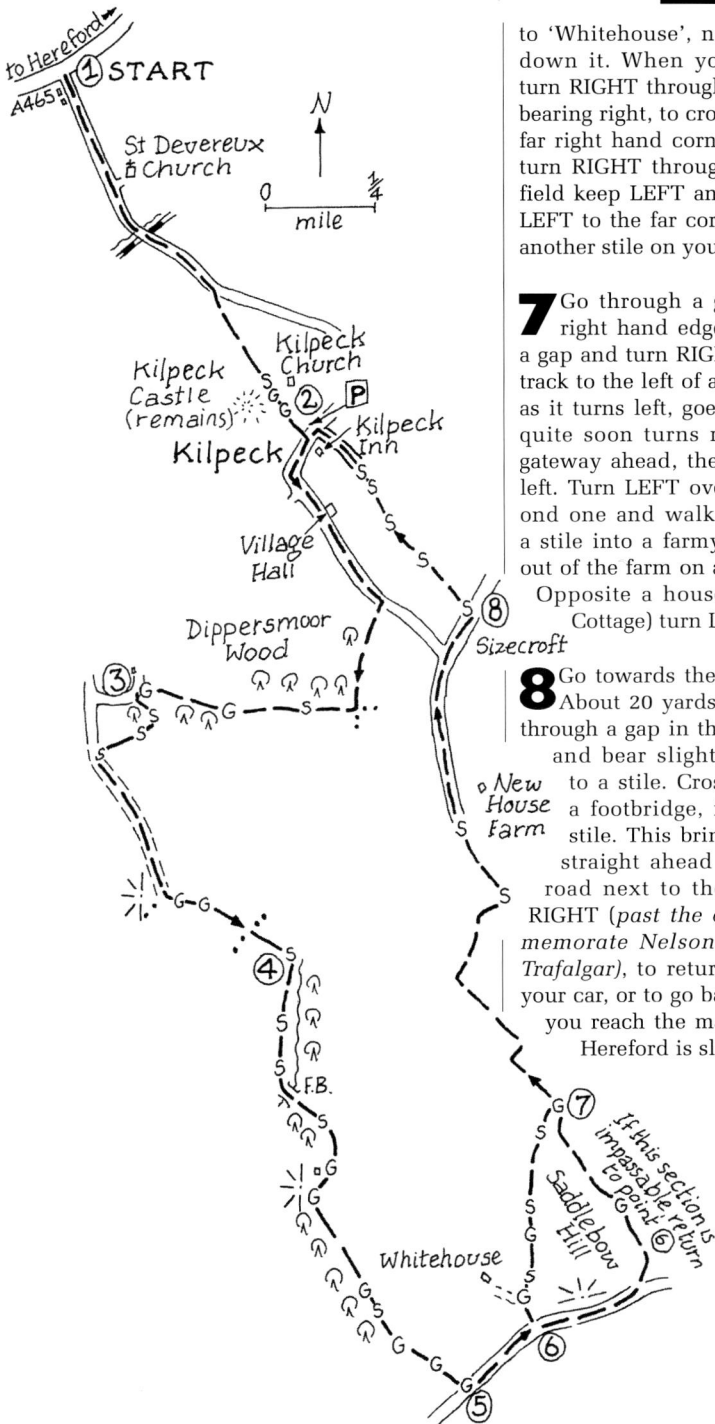

to 'Whitehouse', now on your RIGHT, turn down it. When you reach a gate in front, turn RIGHT through another. Cross the field, bearing right, to cross a stile, then aim for the far right hand corner of the next field. Here turn RIGHT through a gate and in the next field keep LEFT and soon cross a stile. Bear LEFT to the far corner of the field and cross another stile on your right. Turn LEFT.

7 Go through a gate and walk along the right hand edge of a field. Pass through a gap and turn RIGHT along a grassy/muddy track to the left of a hedge. Stay on this track as it turns left, goes through a gateway, and quite soon turns right. When it ends at a gateway ahead, there are two gates on your left. Turn LEFT over a stile next to the second one and walk straight ahead, crossing a stile into a farmyard and then continuing out of the farm on a lane. Pass a left turning. Opposite a house on the right (Sizecroft Cottage) turn LEFT over a stile.

8 Go towards the very bottom of the field. About 20 yards to the left of a corner go through a gap in the trees. Soon cross a stile and bear slightly LEFT down the field to a stile. Cross this and then, in turn, a footbridge, field, stile, paddock and stile. This brings you into a yard. Keep straight ahead along a drive to meet a road next to the pub. Turn LEFT, then RIGHT (*past the oak tree planted to commemorate Nelson's 1805 victory at Cape Trafalgar*), to return to the churchyard and your car, or to go back to the bus stop. When you reach the main road, the bus stop for Hereford is slightly to your RIGHT.

PENGETHLEY, RIVER WYE & SELLACK

DESCRIPTION This is a delightfully varied 8 mile easy walk that includes National Trust parkland, woodland, riverside, views, two interesting churches and a pub, also a café at the end (or start). There are several ascents and descents, but none are very steep.

START Pengethley Manor bus stop (the stop after the turning to Monmouth, coming from Hereford), SO 541256.

DIRECTIONS The 32/33 bus between Hereford and Ross-on-Wye stops here. If using a car, park in a small lay-by on the left a few hundred yards towards Ross after Pengethley Manor, now called Brooks Country House. Then walk very carefully along the verge/pavement past the Manor to the bus stop.

I If coming from Hereford, walk back about 15 yards and turn RIGHT through a kissing gate, then LEFT to walk close to the hedge along the top of Pengethley Park (National Trust parkland, with many ancient oaks and other trees). At the end, go through a gate into woodland and turn RIGHT. At the bottom, turn RIGHT. *Before doing so, you may wish to visit Hentland Church in front of you in its peaceful setting.* Go through a kissing gate back into the park and walk ahead. As you approach a copse, bear slightly RIGHT to pass the trees and a pond on your left.

2 When you reach a hedge/fence and gate in front, don't go through the gate but turn LEFT and walk down to the valley bottom and up the other side just to the right of a wood, through a gate and round to the RIGHT with an orchard to your left. Go through a gate and turn LEFT through two more. Follow the track next to a field on your right. At the first junction, turn LEFT and walk next to the hedge on your right with a row of pylons visible on the left.

3 After about a mile, turn LEFT on a road and walk downhill to a junction on the left. Here turn RIGHT over a stile and walk ahead across the grass to the river. Turn RIGHT and walk along the river bank for about a mile to reach Sellack suspension bridge. *This was built in 1895 to replace the ferry that linked Sellack with Kings Caple on the other side.* Turn RIGHT and walk via a footbridge and two stiles to reach Sellack church wall on the left. Turn RIGHT immediately after the house on the right. *The church on the left is worth a visit; interesting historical information is available inside and there is a renowned gravestone in the churchyard close to the church near the east end of the north aisle (the opposite corner from where you enter the churchyard). It has a finger pointing towards heaven with the word 'GONE'.)*

4 Walk up the track/drive, passing Caradoc Court on your right and going through a farm, with stables on the right and a duck pond on the left. When you reach a road (at the same junction where you joined the road in Section 3), turn LEFT. In a few minutes you will see the Lough Pool Inn ahead on the right.

5 Opposite the turning to Upper Grove Common, turn LEFT through a gate. After a footbridge and another gate, enter a meadow and walk ahead along the bottom of the valley to enter a wood through a gate to the RIGHT of a pool. The narrow path ends at a T junction with another path. Here turn RIGHT uphill; on leaving the wood maintain direction across a field to the corner of a hedge under an oak tree. Keep ahead with the hedge on your left, and maintain your direction when the hedge turns left.

6 Cross a road with a gate each side, then continue across a field to enter a garden

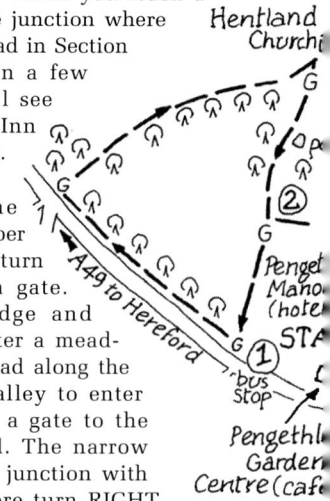

Hentland Church

Penget Manor (hote)

STA

bus Stop

Pengethle Garden Centre (café

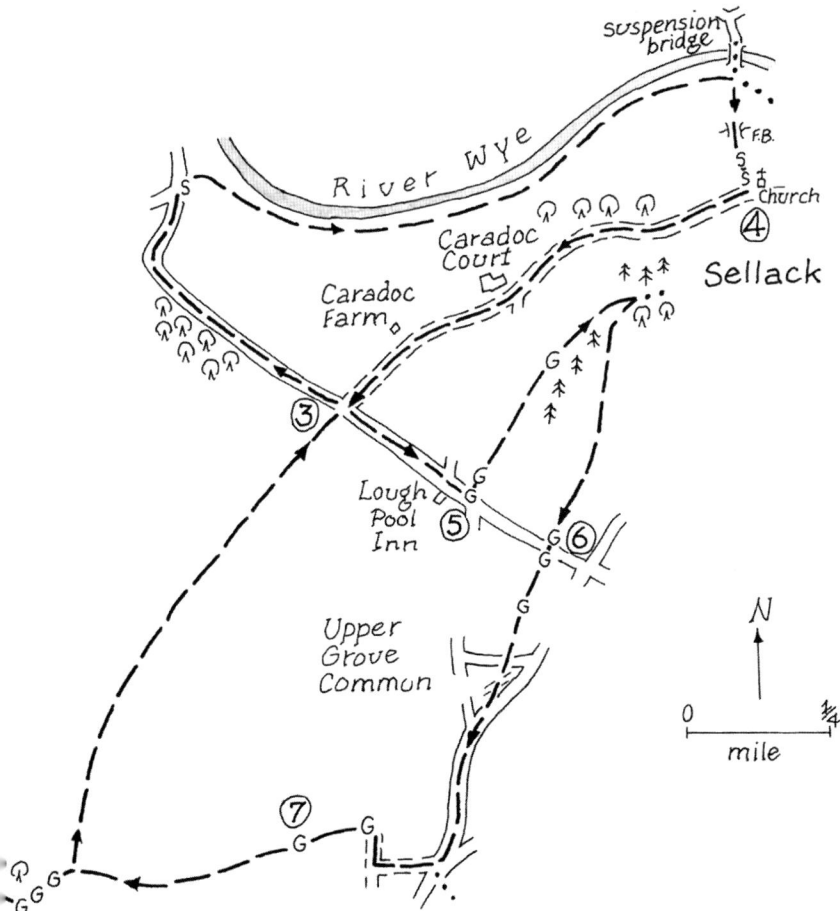

through another gate. Walk straight ahead past the house to your left. Cross a drive and quite soon another. Pass on old fenced-in pump on your right and go through a narrow gap between hedges. At the third drive keep ahead along it to a road. Go ahead along this past a turning on the right and, opposite the first turning on the left, turn RIGHT along a track. At a junction by Tally Ho Cottage turn RIGHT again, then quite soon turn LEFT through a gate. Walk straight up the edge of the field and through another gate.

7 At once turn RIGHT through a gap and LEFT to walk up the next field with the hedge to your left. Continue to the end. Turn LEFT and then RIGHT on the track you came along earlier. Go through two gates, then turn RIGHT through another. (If you came by car, it's easier not to turn right here but to walk ahead all the way to the main road. Then turn LEFT back to your car.) Follow the route you used earlier round to the left, down the valley and a little way up the other side to the gate which is now on your left. Turn LEFT through this and walk uphill with Pengethley Manor over on your left. Return to the start via the kissing gate. If you need refreshment before catching the bus, walk carefully along the verge past the entrance to the hotel to Pengethley Garden Centre, where there is a welcoming café.

WALK 4
KING'S THORN & ATHELSTAN'S WOOD

DESCRIPTION This is a 6½ mile moderate walk through very attractive countryside and woodland with some excellent views. It visits an ancient wood, a couple of interesting churches, an old holy well and a later version of the thorn that the village of King's Thorn is named after.
START King's Thorn bus shelter, SO 498322.
DIRECTIONS The 32/33 bus between Hereford and Ross-on-Wye stops at King's Thorn, by the turning to Little Birch. There is a small car parking area next to the shelter.

1 Walk carefully down the minor road (called 'The Thorn') opposite the bus shelter, signed towards Little Birch. Opposite Wrigglebrook Lane turn LEFT up a track. At a cross tracks turn RIGHT. When you reach a gate ahead leading into the wood, turn RIGHT in front of it. Continue on the track as far as a road next to a Methodist Chapel. Cross over and keep ahead (don't fork left) down a tree lined path. Ignore turnings off this path/track. Soon after 'Saddlebow View' a road joins from the right.

2 Just after 'Bwthyn Tir Glas' keep ahead through a gate and gently downhill. Cross a farm track and an old stile to walk next to a plantation of young trees on your left. *This is Athelstan's Wood, an ancient wood dating back to Saxon times. It has some impressive conifers, and is now owned by the Duchy of Cornwall, with an increasing number of broadleaved trees.* At the next junction turn LEFT and follow the track downhill. Ignore a waymarked path to the left but stay on the track as it swings round to the right, soon with a stream on your left (not always easily seen). Continue to the right of the stream past a left turning and at a fork keep left, staying close to the stream. Leave the wood over a stile ahead and soon reach a road. Turn LEFT.

3 When you reach a farm the road turns left but you keep ahead through the left hand gate into the yard. Bear LEFT on a permissive route through the farm to exit by turning RIGHT through a gateway into a field to the left of a barn. Keep along the right hand side of the field to leave it through a gate. Turn RIGHT through another gate, then sharp LEFT along a track next to a hedge. Follow the track round to the left and then keep ahead with a stream to your right (don't be tempted to cross it), emerging into a meadow. Keep close to the trees on your right, crossing a stile and then, later, another. Turn LEFT uphill to cross a third stile just to the right of a large ash tree (if still there). Turn RIGHT on the road.

4 Turn LEFT at the next junction. You may wish to make a short diversion by turning RIGHT to Little Dewchurch church; *its tower is medieval but the rest was designed by the famous Victorian architect Frederick Preedy. The churchyard is a pleasant place for a break, and contains an attractive old cherry tree in the far right hand corner.* Afterwards return to the junction, and keep RIGHT. When the tarmac ends, keep ahead up the grassy track past a stile. Soon pass two more, then keep to the left hand side of one field and straight across another to re-enter Athelstan's Wood over a stile. The path descends to a T junction, then turns LEFT to a little plateau. Turn RIGHT down steps to cross a plank bridge over a stream. After a short climb, turn LEFT, then RIGHT up the track you came down earlier.

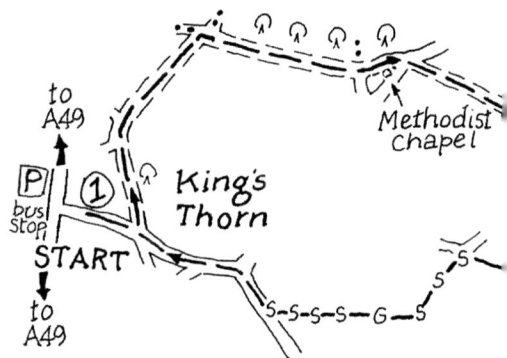

5 At the next junction take the second turning on the RIGHT (not the path you used earlier). Leave the wood over a stile and keep along the left hand edge of the field to its far left corner, where you re-enter the wood. The clear path soon bears RIGHT, then later bears

apparently a local landowner who didn't like people visiting the well and so blocked it up; the water then came up into his own house, so he re-opened the well.) Go up an often muddy track on stepping stones. At the top turn RIGHT up another track. At the road turn LEFT, then RIGHT at the T junction. Very soon after passing a turning to the right, bear LEFT up a grassy track.

7 *Just before a junction to houses you will see, if you look carefully, a small Hawthorn tree on your right and a plaque*

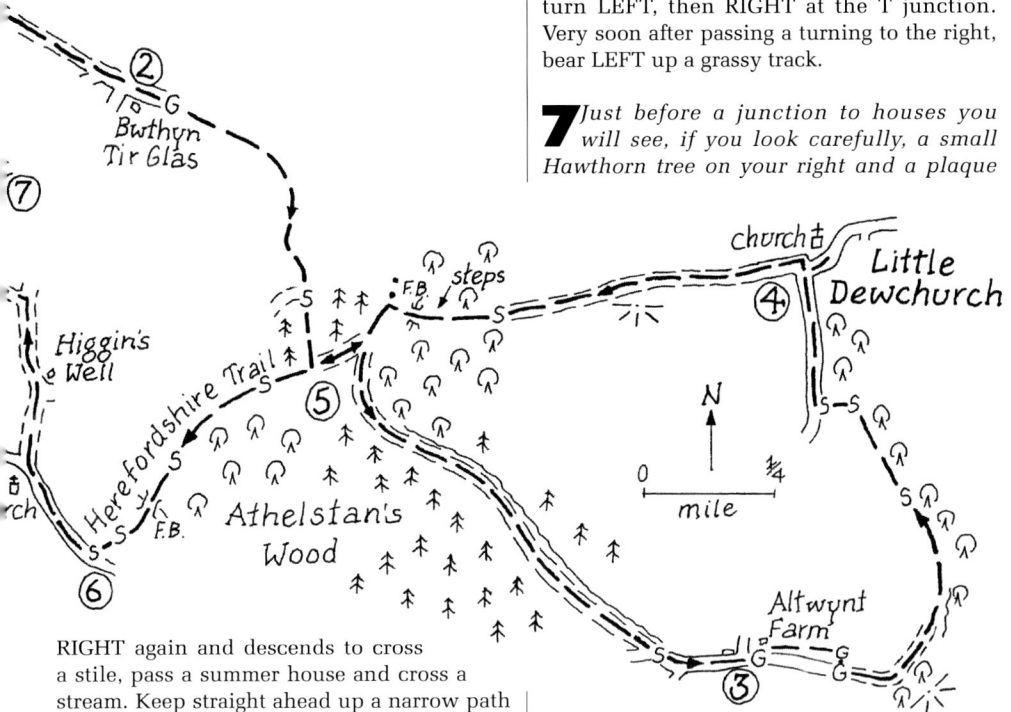

RIGHT again and descends to cross a stile, pass a summer house and cross a stream. Keep straight ahead up a narrow path to a meadow and, before reaching a house, turn RIGHT to cross a stile. Turn LEFT to walk past the house to a stile taking you to a lane.

6 Turn RIGHT. Soon you reach Little Birch church – *another interesting Victorian church, entirely paid for by the rector in 1869 at a cost of £3600, and with a beautiful wrought iron screen.* Just after the church, turn RIGHT down an unsigned stony track and at the bottom turn LEFT past Higgins Well. *(Go through the gate by the well if you want to see the plaque; it is said to be an old sacred well and was restored for Queen Victoria's diamond jubilee. Higgins was*

(hard to read) identifying it as raised from a graft of the Holy Thorn (at Glastonbury). Continue up past the junction and at the road turn LEFT over a stile and soon another to pass a house and go through a gate. Turn LEFT and at the end of the track cross a stile ahead into a field. Turn RIGHT. Walk along the edge of two fields separated by a gate, then cross a stile onto a path which takes you to a track. Turn LEFT, then RIGHT over a stile and go ahead near the bottom of a field to another stile on the LEFT by a telegraph pole. Cross this to a road. Turn RIGHT, then take the next LEFT turning. Ignore side roads to return to the start.

KING'S THORN TO HEREFORD

DESCRIPTION This is a 8 mile moderate linear walk, with a regular bus service to the start. It includes some beautiful and remote countryside, two wooded iron age hill forts and a quiet route back to Hereford, avoiding busy roads and including a stretch by the river Wye. There is a steady climb to the top of the first hill fort, and a shorter but steeper climb up the second, but the rest of the walk is downhill or on the flat.
START King's Thorn bus shelter, SO 498322.
FINISH Hereford Cathedral, SO 510398.
DIRECTIONS The 32/33 bus between Hereford and Ross-on-Wye stops at King's Thorn, by the turning to Little Birch.

I Walk down the minor road opposite the bus shelter and opposite Wrigglebrook Lane turn LEFT up a track. At a cross tracks turn RIGHT. Go through a gate into Aconbury Wood and in about 80 yards, just as the track starts to descend, fork RIGHT gently uphill. Fork LEFT at the next junction, then ignore turnings and pass through a gap in the hillfort ramparts. At a T junction turn RIGHT. Ignore a right turning but soon after this keep LEFT up to a trig point. Continue through the ramparts and immediately turn RIGHT and soon LEFT away from the ramparts. When the path divides, take either as they soon join up again. At a junction with a larger track turn LEFT. Ignore turnings and continue straight down to the edge of the wood. Turn RIGHT; cross a stile

and then turn LEFT over another to leave the wood.

2 Walk down the left hand edge of the field, soon re-entering woodland over two stiles. Turn LEFT. On reaching a stony track turn RIGHT and very soon LEFT down a grassy path. Exit the wood and walk ahead straight down the field, passing a wooded area on your left, to reach a road. Turn RIGHT, passing a pond, Aconbury Court and Aconbury Church (closed, but with two interesting wooden carved figures in the porch). Turn LEFT at the T-junction and in about 500 yards turn RIGHT over a stile.

3 Head across the field past a solitary oak tree, then continue past a stile to walk close to the wood on your right. The path crosses a double stile, then passes a footbridge on the right and crosses another stile. About 300 yards later, just past a small group of trees, the route bends slightly LEFT to a stile. Cross this and continue ahead to the far left corner of the field to go through a gate to reach a long drive. Keep ahead along this past a new house and across a stream. The drive eventually turns left to reach a road. Here turn RIGHT.

4 In a minute or two look for a stile on your LEFT. Cross this and walk ahead uphill and over another stile. At the top corner bear RIGHT over a third stile tucked away in the undergrowth and turn RIGHT to walk next to the hedge. When you reach a stile, don't cross it but turn LEFT steeply uphill next to the hedge. Turn LEFT in front of the next stile along a permissive route and soon turn RIGHT through a gate into a wood, entering Dinedor hill fort.

5 Turn LEFT at the T junction and bear RIGHT through the trees, aiming for the opposite diagonal corner from where you

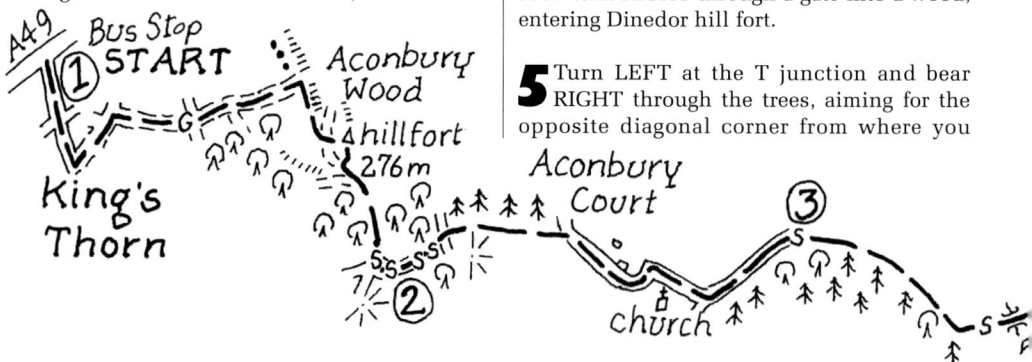

10

entered. Look for a handrail guiding you down to a road and a noticeboard about the site. (If you get lost, there is a path all the way round near the edge of the fort which will take you to the handrail in no more than 10 minutes.) Turn RIGHT and then, next to a Dinedor Parish Council map, LEFT down a permissive path. Turn LEFT at a junction by a beech tree. At a T junction turn LEFT past a gate to a road. Turn RIGHT, then RIGHT again down a no through road.

6 Fork LEFT in a few minutes down a smaller track and soon turn RIGHT along a narrow path in front of a gate. Enter a field through a gate and leave through another gate a little way down on the right. Go half-LEFT to cross a stile and then turn RIGHT to walk round the edge of the orchard. Leave through a gate just to the left of the bottom right hand corner (don't go into the next field), then after another gate turn LEFT to walk through the underpass. Turn LEFT through a gate, and after another gate walk past a yard and pond on your right. The path goes next to a hedge on your right and quite soon goes through a gap so that the hedge is now on your left. Turn RIGHT next to a stream. After two more gates reach a road.

7 Turn LEFT. At the junction turn RIGHT to reach a main road. Cross with care, turn RIGHT to cross the stream, and immediately LEFT to walk to the left of St Elizabeth's Cottages to reach, and go next to, the river Wye. The path goes through a gate; by the old locked bridge on your left, bear RIGHT to reach some interesting metal sculptures (with information board) and the Greenway cycle path. Turn LEFT and cross the new (2013) bridge. Turn LEFT and in about 25 yards bear RIGHT down a narrow path to a gate leading into a meadow.

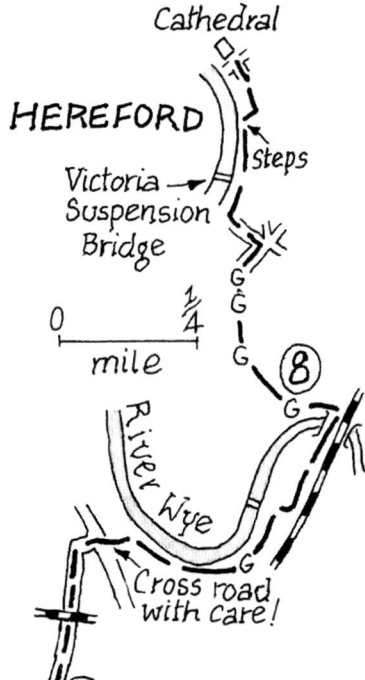

8 Walk across to a gate in the middle of a hedge. Once through this, continue in the same direction to the far corner of the field. Go through two gates to reach a road. Turn RIGHT. Take the next turning on the LEFT (Vicarage Road); at the end continue down a narrow passage next to a wall and round to the right next to the river. When the path ends, walk ahead, with the Victoria suspension bridge (*1898*) to your left, up steps and then along the green, looking over the river to your left. At the end, pass the building on your left and walk down a slope. Walk ahead on the road to a T junction. Turn LEFT to reach the cathedral.

VOWCHURCH & POSTON

DESCRIPTION This is a varied 5½ mile walk including woods, meadows, some delightful views and constantly changing scenery. There is a steep climb at the start, and a shorter one later on.
START Bus stop at Vowchurch Turn, SO 364368.
DIRECTIONS The 39 (39A on Sundays) bus between Hereford and Hay-on-Wye goes via Vowchurch Turn. If coming by car, turn left off the B4348 (signed to Vowchurch) at the crossroads at Vowchurch Turn; in about 200 yards park in a little lay-by opposite the church (not on Sunday if there is a service).

I Walk up the No Through road signed to Vowchurch Common. Just after 'Hillside' on the right, bear LEFT on a stony track. Follow this round to the left and continue on it as it eventually becomes a grassy/muddy path. Immediately after a stile on the left, turn RIGHT up a steep path, soon forking LEFT. Continue steeply up, and over the drive to 'Quercwm'. When you reach a road, turn RIGHT downhill. Just after the former Myrtle Cottage (*currently being renovated*), turn LEFT along a tarmac track, which soon becomes grassy. Stay on this until it eventually ascends to a T junction by a house on the right.

2 Turn LEFT up the lane. As you approach a house, turn sharply LEFT through a gate towards a large green barn. Follow the drive round to the right and ahead through a gate to a delightful grassy plateau with a picnic bench (provided for walkers by the benevolent landowner). *Straight ahead there is a good view of Ysgyryd Fawr (The Skirrid) with its second lower peak arising from a landslip.* Turn RIGHT though a gate and walk along the narrow path, over a stile and through a gate. Immediately after this, turn RIGHT. Before long, go through a gate to reach a road. Turn RIGHT and immediately LEFT over a stile. Go straight across the field and through a gate into some woodland, which you soon leave over a stile. After crossing another stile in front of you, bear slightly LEFT steeply downhill to a footbridge and stile. Cross these, walk straight up the next field and look for a hidden footbridge and stile on your left leading into the wood. Cross these and climb up to, and over, a stile leading out of the wood.

3 Turn LEFT and walk along the top of the field with good views over the Wye Valley to your right. Near the end of the field, fork LEFT through trees and then walk past a large house and lawn on your right. Soon turn LEFT off the track in front of trees and very soon cross a stile hidden in the hedge on your RIGHT. Keep along the left hand edge of the field to leave over a stile in the corner. Go ahead past a house on your right and through a gate to the right of a barn. Keep ahead past buildings on the right and along the track, through a gate and onwards. Just before reaching a road junction, turn RIGHT along a grassy track to the right of a house.

4 Keep ahead into a wood. Ignore a right turn and soon fork LEFT at a waymark post. Your narrow path now wends its way through the wood, sometimes becoming rather faint but not disappearing altogether. Eventually it bends to the left through a damp patch and emerges onto a much larger path. Turn LEFT. Follow the track round to the left and through a gate. Immediately after a tennis court, turn LEFT and soon cross a stile by a gate, with an excellent view of the renowned Poston House (*built in the 18thC and recently restored*) on the right.

5 Keep ahead just to the left of the valley on your right and soon cross a stile into woodland and descend steeply to cross another stile into a wide valley. Go down this but keep to the right hand side of it and well before the bottom bear RIGHT along a narrow path just to the left of a large oak tree, with a view down to the roof of the house on your left. Go through a gate and round to the right. Look for a stile in the hedge ahead fairly near the top of the field. Cross this and keep ahead through a gate. Turn RIGHT over

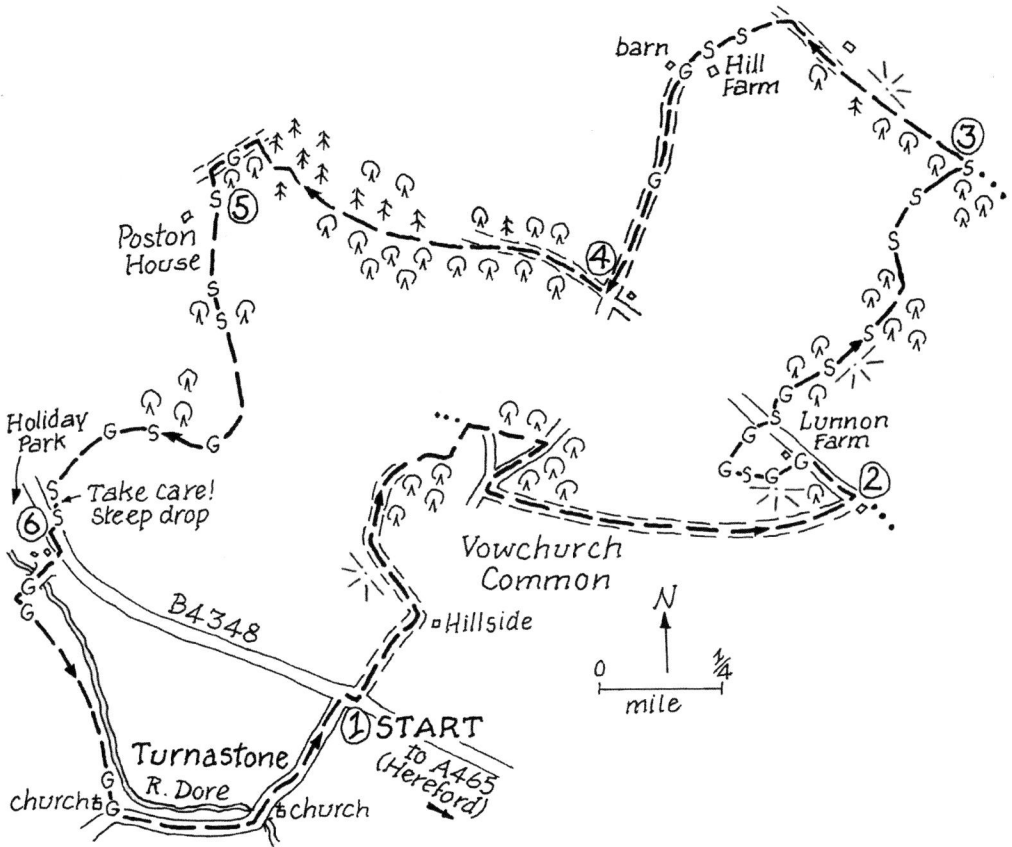

a cattle grid. Turn LEFT and walk straight down the slope, ignoring a stile over on your right. At the fence, turn LEFT and soon cross a stile on your RIGHT – take care here as there is a steep drop immediately after the stile. Descend to cross another stile leading to a busy road.

6 Cross this with great care and turn LEFT. Go past the entrance to The Mill (*refreshments available here if open*) and turn RIGHT into Poston Country Holiday Park. Walk past the reception building (*ice creams available here*) and on to cross a footbridge over the river. Go through a gate and at once turn LEFT through another. Keep along the edge of the field close to the river until you come to a gate in front of you. Go through this and bear RIGHT away from the river to go through another gate leading to a road. *Immediately on your right is Turnastone Church, a simple but beautiful building dating from the 13thC. A little further down the road on your right, on the left hand side, is the oldest operating petrol filling station in Britain, still dispensing petrol (in 2016) from the left hand pump. There is a tiny shop there too, which may be open if you're lucky. Turn LEFT and walk back to Vowchurch and the bus stop. The road passes St. Bartholomew's Church at Vowchurch, in a peaceful setting by the river. It's worth a visit, and has a small permanent exhibition about Skeffington Dodgson (Lewis Carroll's brother), who was vicar here.*

13

EATON CAMP, RUCKHALL & THE CAGE BROOK

DESCRIPTION This is a very pretty 5½ mile moderate walk through some little known countryside close to Hereford. The walk goes to the Iron Age hill fort of Eaton Camp with a commanding view over the River Wye, then goes along a narrow path high above the river for a while and finally returns to the start via an attractive little stream called the Cage Brook.

START Birch Hill Road bus stop, Clehonger, SO 451377.

DIRECTIONS Both the 39 bus (39A on Sundays) between Hereford and Hay-on-Wye and the 449 between Hereford and Madley go via Clehonger. Road parking is possible on Birch Hill Road or on Gosmore Road, which crosses Birch Hill Road. Birch Hill Road is a turning off the B4349 on the left, coming from Hereford.

1 From the bus stop, walk down to the main road, cross over with care, and turn RIGHT. After the first house turn LEFT through a gate into a meadow. Descend this but turn half-RIGHT near the bottom to a gate in the far corner. Once through this keep next to the hedge on the left. Go through a gate into woodland, and then on through two more gates and down steps to cross a footbridge with a gate at the end. Keep ahead for about 15 yards and then turn RIGHT up through two more gates. Bear slightly LEFT and walk near the thicket and later the fence on your left. Leave the field through a gate ahead and at the first corner of the next field turn LEFT through another gate to a road. Turn RIGHT.

2 Turn through the second gate on the LEFT. Bear LEFT across the meadow to another gate. Go through this and keep to the left hand side of the field. About half way down fork LEFT through a gate and

walk downhill to go through another gate next to a house (Tuck Mill) on your left. Continue downhill past another house and over a bridge to a T junction. Turn LEFT. Soon fork RIGHT through a kissing gate and follow the path uphill. About 50 yards after going through a gate, turn RIGHT up steps and through a gate into Eaton Camp hillfort (information board by entrance).

3 Bear RIGHT to walk diagonally over the top of the camp to the far left hand corner. Go through a gate(way) ahead and on down to go through a gate at the far end of the camp; this leads to an excellent viewpoint over the sylvan Wye (and a convenient bench). Turn back through the gate and soon turn RIGHT through a gap and down a rough track to the right. At the bottom turn sharp LEFT and walk close to the river. Cross a stile and continue on the narrow path up and down steps. Take care here as some of the path is not fenced and there is a very steep drop to your right. At a junction of paths in front of a house, turn RIGHT down more steps and cross a stile into a meadow. Keep close to the river, cross another stile and continue via a footbridge. *If you can't continue because the path is too overgrown ahead, turn back over the stile into the meadow and follow section **4b** below. If the path is clear, follow section **4a**.*

4a The path eventually reaches a grassy patch in front of a house. Turn LEFT past a barrier and up a track, continuing in the same direction when the track meets a tarmac lane. When you reach a T junction, turn LEFT. In a few hundred yards, turn LEFT over a stile by a rough track. Soon keep ahead into the left hand field through a gate. Keep along the right hand edge and fork RIGHT over a footbridge to rejoin the track by turning LEFT. The track becomes a path, bends slightly to the LEFT and crosses a stile and a stone stile to lead onto a drive/road. Walk ahead. Later, pass a left turn by a small green.

4b If riverside path is blocked: After turning back over the stile into the meadow, turn half-RIGHT past a small oak tree to reach a stile by a gate. Cross this, go up a track over a cross paths to reach a road and turn RIGHT. Take the next LEFT turning.

5 At a T junction, turn LEFT, then keep RIGHT. Go downhill to another T junction and turn RIGHT. Soon turn LEFT over a stile by a gate. The following section often has temporary wire fencing which you have to go under or over. Walk ahead across the grass to walk with the brook on your left. Cross a stile and now keep just to the right of trees. Pass a footbridge on the left, then cross a stile ahead. Just in front of a fenced area on your left, turn LEFT over a stile, then RIGHT over another. Bear LEFT down to the brook and walk next to it for some way. Cross a footbridge ahead (over an often dry tributary) and continue past a house to reach a road.

6 Cross this very carefully (blind bend), turn LEFT for a short way, then RIGHT through a gate. Almost at once turn LEFT over a plank bridge and up steps. Turn RIGHT over a stile, then LEFT to go straight up the meadow to pass through a gap in the hedge ahead, then on to a stile at the end of the field, about half-way across. This leads to a narrow path to the right of a house. A final stile brings you to a road – a busy one so take care. Cross over, turn RIGHT, and then LEFT along Poplar road. Turn LEFT along The Hollies, then RIGHT at the next T junction. Soon turn LEFT at the end of Syers Croft and RIGHT along Gosmore Road. The second turning on the LEFT is Birch Hill Road, where you started.

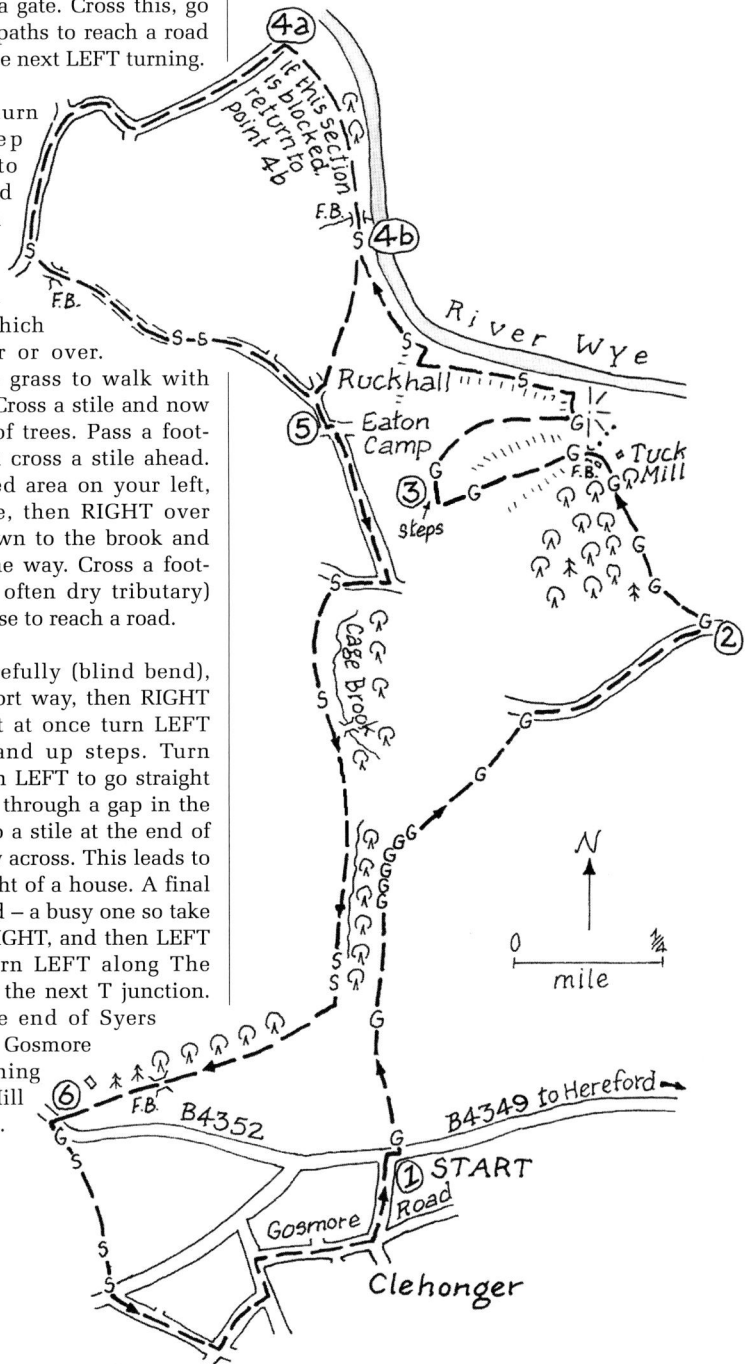

If this section is blocked, return to point 4b

F.B.

4b

River Wye

Ruckhall

Eaton Camp

Tuck Mill

F.B.

steps

Cage Brook

N

0   ¼ mile

B4352

B4349 to Hereford

START Road

Gosmore

Clehonger

CAPLER CAMP & THE WYE

DESCRIPTION This 5 mile walk is moderate on the whole, though it involves one short steep climb. It goes across country at first, through attractive undulating countryside, and then climbs up to the impressive Iron Age hill fort of Capler Camp. There is then a section next to the river Wye, followed by a gentle ascent above the river before a descent back to Fownhope.

START Cross-roads immediately before Fownhope Church, coming from Hereford, SO 581343. If coming by car, park at Fownhope recreation field, SO 579341.

DIRECTIONS The 453 and 454 buses run between Hereford and Fownhope. Alight at the Church Croft bus stop, soon after the bus turns left at the cross-roads by the church; then walk back down to the cross-roads. If coming by car from Hereford, turn RIGHT at the cross-roads by Fownhope Church down Capler Lane, then look for a narrow turning signed to the Recreation Field. Turn RIGHT along this, and park beyond the pavilion. Walk back to the road and turn RIGHT. Then ignore the first two sentences of Section 1.

1 From the cross-roads by the church, walk along Capler Lane, with the church on your left. Pass the turning to the Recreation Field on your right. Immediately before 'Pippins' on the right, turn LEFT up the drive of Ring House. When level with the house, and just in front of a garage with three openings, turn LEFT up a short concrete patch through a gate and on up ahead, going through another gate and soon over a stile. After ascending a short steep bank, turn LEFT. Cross a stile and keep ahead until you reach an old wall in front of you.

2 Turn RIGHT and walk along the edge of a field with the wall to your left. Continue down the field, bearing slightly LEFT, and as you approach the bottom keep parallel with and to the left of a line of trees. Pass a grassy

mound and look for a bridge over a stream. Cross this and keep ahead (do not turn right) uphill; continue in the same direction possibly with a fence to your right – though this may be temporary. At the top of the field cross a stile ahead. Then bear very slightly LEFT to cross another stile and continue in the same direction down the field. At the bottom turn RIGHT. Pass an overgrown stile and soon turn LEFT over a stile and across a little stream (which may be dry). Now keep next to the hedge on your right.

3 Before long turn RIGHT with the hedge and go through a gate. At once turn LEFT. Soon turn LEFT over a stile; keep ahead across a field and walk through a gap. Then turn RIGHT to walk below a wooded enclosure to your left. Cross a stile ahead and then aim for the far right hand end of the field. Go through a gate on your RIGHT, and now bear LEFT to the top corner of this field. Go through a gate and walk past caravans and buildings to emerge in a yard. Pass a large barn on your left, cross the drive and enter a field.

4 Turn RIGHT, pass a house on your right, go through a gate, a field and another gate, and then climb steeply up to a stile. Then keep RIGHT. Pass a tall wooden post marking the entrance to Capler hill fort. Walk to the far LEFT hand end of the fort, going down into the ditch to join a path leaving through a gate. Quite soon bear LEFT as waymarked through conifers and soon LEFT again down a track to a road. (Your route turns right here, but a few yards to your left there is a lovely viewpoint over the Wye, a bench, some wooden carvings and an interesting noticeboard.) Turn RIGHT to walk carefully down the road. Opposite a small layby turn sharply LEFT down a track and very soon fork RIGHT down a steep narrow path.

5 At the bottom, turn RIGHT over a stile and walk by the river. The riverside route crosses a footbridge and a stile, goes through two gates and finally crosses a stile to enter a small garden. Cross this to leave over another stile. Leave the river now by bearing RIGHT

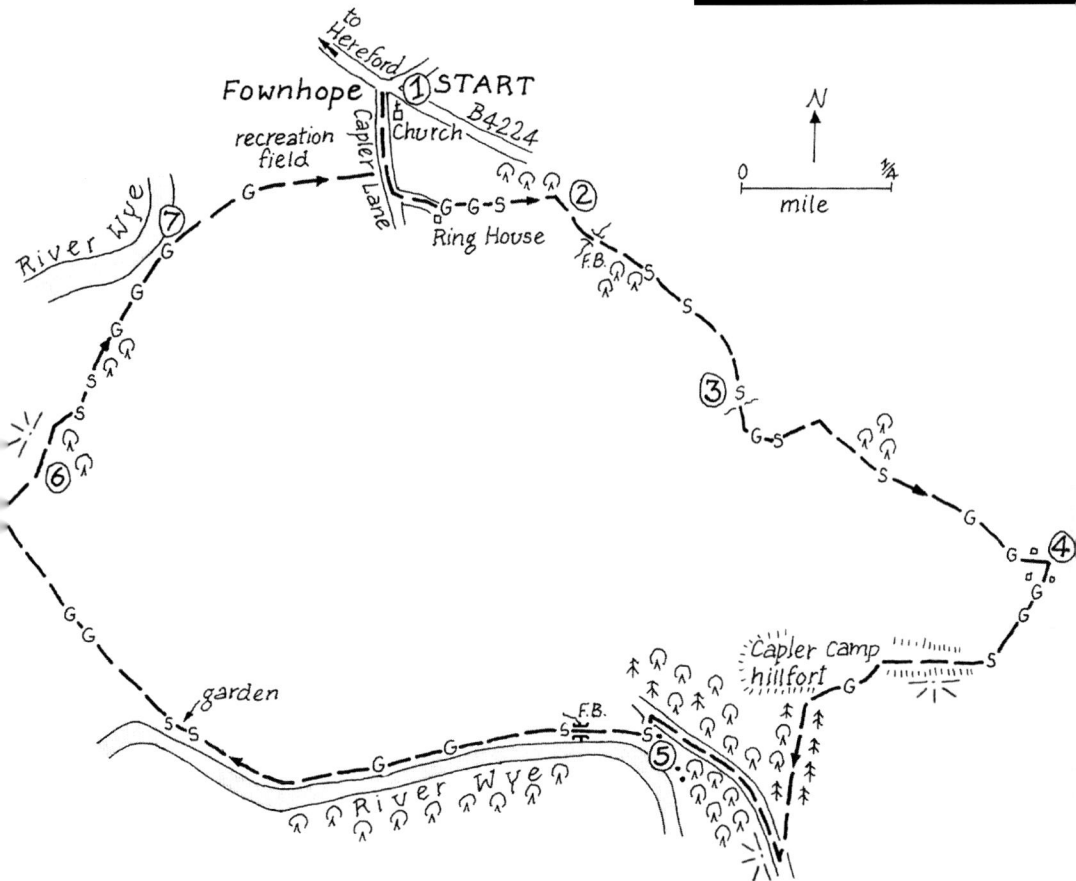

to go along the top of the field to the far right corner. Go through a double gate and a kissing gate and across a plank bridge. Continue ahead, before long with a hedge next to you on your right. When you reach a stile next to a large gate on your RIGHT, cross this and walk up the right hand edge of the field. Just after passing an oak tree by a metal gate, bear LEFT across the field towards an old barn.

6 Pass this, keeping it to your right, and keep ahead. Ignore a turning on the right leading to another field. Cross a stile by a gate, then soon another. Head half right to a kissing gate to the left of some large trees. Go through this and bear slightly RIGHT towards the bottom left hand corner of the field. About 50 yards before the corner, turn LEFT down a short steep path to go through

a gate. Continue down and round to the right down steps to pass through the edge of a garden overlooking the river and emerge in a grassy area next to a weeping willow.

7 Turn LEFT through a gate, and then RIGHT to walk away from the river. As the hedge bends left, turn RIGHT through a gate onto the recreation field. Keep RIGHT to return to your car if you drove here; if not, walk past the pavilion and children's playground and onto a tarmac lane to your right. This leads to a road. Turn LEFT to return to the cross-roads by the church. Turn LEFT to get to the pubs, village shop and bus stops. (The bus takes a circular route through the village, so you can catch it at any bus stop to return to Hereford.)

NUPEND WOOD & CHERRY HILL

DESCRIPTION This 5 mile walk is a pleasant mixture of open country and delightful woodland, including the ancient sloping Nupend Wood, one of Hereford Wildlife Trust's reserves, and Cherry Hill Iron Age hill fort. There is a short steep climb in the reserve, but the other ascents are more gentle.

START Church Croft bus stop, Fownhope, SO 582345. If coming by car, park at Fownhope recreation field, SO 579341.

DIRECTIONS The 453 and 454 buses run between Hereford and Fownhope; alight at Church Croft, which is the first stop after the bus turns left by the church. If coming by car from Hereford, turn RIGHT at the cross-roads by Fownhope Church and then look for a narrow turning signed to the Recreation Field. Turn RIGHT along this, and park beyond the pavilion. Then walk back to the church, cross over the main road with care and walk up Common Hill Lane; then take the next turning on the LEFT, Church Croft.

I Immediately after the bus shelter on the left in Church Croft, bear RIGHT up a grassy track. As the path starts to descend, turn LEFT over a stile. Cross the field to leave over another stile about three quarters of the way along. Climb up to a cross-tracks.

2 Turn LEFT and walk down the track to a road. Cross this and then descend over a stream. Go through a gate ahead, and soon go up a few steps on your RIGHT to enter Nupend Wood past a Herefordshire Wildlife Trust noticeboard. Climb steadily up a fairly steep path with steps, eventually flattening off, then ascending again to pass through a tall gate to leave the reserve.

3 Quite soon re-enter the reserve by turning LEFT through another (normal) gate; follow the path steeply down and round to the left, passing a grassy meadow on your right (awash with flowers in summer). Turn LEFT down some steps; then turn RIGHT and follow the winding path, which bears RIGHT down through the meadow to leave the reserve onto a track. Turn LEFT, walk past the entrance to the reserve and back through the gate. Turn LEFT.

4 Join the Wye Valley Walk (WVW) by forking LEFT through a gate; walk up a stony track, soon entering a meadow. As the track peters out, keep ahead across the grass and over a stile, then next to a hedge on your right. Continue on a good track, going through a gate and past Hope Springs Farm and holiday cottage. At the next junction turn LEFT. (Here you can make a short diversion by keeping ahead instead of turning left; in about 80 yards you can see on your right an old quarry, now a geological SSSI, and a lime kiln. After looking at these go back to the junction, and turn RIGHT.)

5 Just after Bagpiper Cottage fork LEFT (leaving the WVW). The lane becomes tarmacked and passes a turning up to the left. About 135 yards after the turning, turn up a narrow unsigned path on the LEFT going up over a muddy bank a few feet high. Continue up through the trees to reach a T junction with a wider stony track. Turn LEFT. Keep going for some way, ascending gently, and passing an old bench. When the path forks, keep LEFT downhill, soon crossing another track and then rising again quite steeply. At the next fork keep LEFT along the side of the ridge. The next section is quite tricky, but stay parallel to and just below the ridge on your right, eventually rising up to the ridge.

6 When you reach a waymarked crossing of paths, turn RIGHT down steps and at the next junction turn LEFT. Ignore right turns but at the next cross-paths turn RIGHT as waymarked. The next stretch is often muddy but gets drier as it rises. Bear LEFT to walk through an old hill fort. The path then descends gently; when you reach a little oak tree dividing the path in two, turn RIGHT down a narrow path. At the bottom of the wood turn RIGHT and at once LEFT past a stile. Bear LEFT down the road and cross over the main road at West End Stores. There is a bus stop for Hereford on your

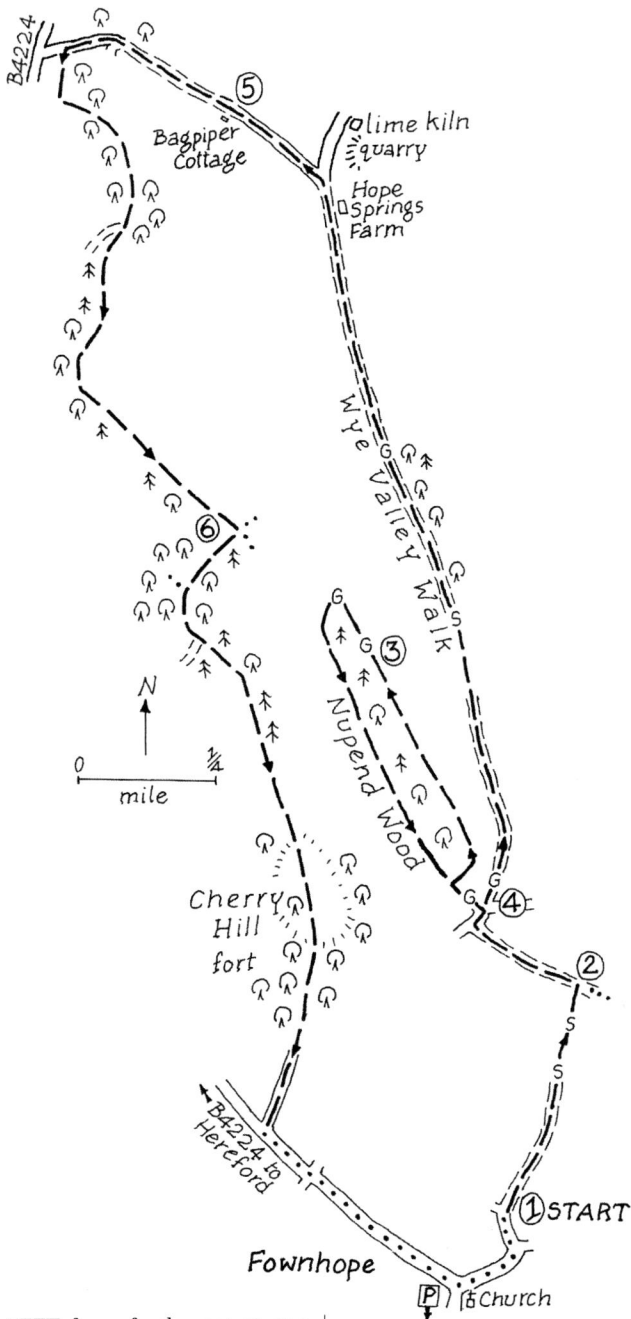

B4224

⑤

lime kiln
quarry

Bagpiper
Cottage

Hope
Springs
Farm

Wye Valley Walk

⑥

N

0 ¼
mile

Nupend Wood

③

④

②

Cherry
Hill
fort

B4224 to
Hereford

Fownhope

①START

P to Church

right, or turn LEFT for refreshment at one
of the two pubs or to reach the church and
return to the car park.

WALK 10

HAUGH WOOD, WESSINGTON & COMMON HILL

DESCRIPTION This is a beautiful 8 mile moderate walk through remote Herefordshire countryside and woodland, which takes in five nature reserves, with many woodland and meadow flowers to be seen in spring and summer.
START & DIRECTIONS Same as for **Walk 9**.

1 Follow Section **1** of **Walk 9**.

2 Keep ahead past a house on your right. Follow the path round to the right and then downhill to go through a gate to walk through a tree plantation. Exit via a gate to a road. Turn RIGHT and soon LEFT through a gate. Walk ahead, crossing a footbridge and going through a gate onto a track. Turn LEFT. Pass a stile on the left and then, just before a cattle grid, turn RIGHT up a path which winds up into the wood. In a few minutes the path turns right up to a forest track. Turn LEFT, and soon RIGHT up a narrow path. At once fork LEFT, then very soon LEFT again; the path becomes wider and clearer as it passes a garden on the left. Continue through two gates and a pasture to reach a road. Cross this, go through a gate and over a footbridge and a stile. Go to the far RIGHT corner of the field to enter a wood via a gate. Turn LEFT, then very soon RIGHT along a narrow path down, then up to emerge onto a track.

3 Turn RIGHT and soon keep to the left of a gate. Enter the wood through a gate and follow the path round to the right, and up a sunken track. Ignore left turnings and near the top ignore a right fork and reach a wide forest track. Turn LEFT, then at once RIGHT and immediately LEFT on a path. Keep on the main path to a T-junction with a meadow now visible to the right. Turn RIGHT and pass through a gate into the meadow. *You are now in Joan's Hill Farm Reserve, owned by Plantlife.* Keep ahead with a thicket on your left and then on into the next field, now with a hedge on your right. Cross a stile and turn LEFT; at the bottom turn RIGHT. Go through a gate and at the end of the next field turn LEFT down through a gateway into another field. *Between May and July it's worth making a short detour by turning RIGHT at the end of the field up to see all the wild flowers in the meadow, and there is an information board at the top.*

4 At the far right hand corner go through a gate and turn LEFT. Cross a footbridge and bear slightly LEFT towards a house. Cross a stile and pass the house on your left. Keep ahead down the lane to reach a junction. Turn RIGHT and RIGHT again at the next junction. Where the lane bends right, cross a stile on the LEFT. Keep along the right hand edge of the field, cross a footbridge and again bear RIGHT. When the fence turns right, keep ahead across the field to the far corner. Cross a stile and footbridge and walk ahead (indistinct path) to a gate into another field. Keep along the right edge and at the end turn RIGHT through a gate to walk along the left hand side of a field. At the end, enter the wood through a gate.

5 Keep ahead over a ditch/stream and up near the stream on your left (no path). Turn LEFT on a track. This passes a house and becomes very stony, soon turning left up to a drive. Turn RIGHT. When you reach a road, cross it and walk ahead across the grass (you are now on Broadmoor Common, a local nature reserve of flower-rich ancient grassland) to reach another road, where you bear LEFT. When the road starts to bend to the right, turn LEFT over an old cattle grid (no waymark in 2017) and bear RIGHT across the field to the right of a small pond surrounded by trees. Pass through a gate and go to the far RIGHT corner of the field. Enter woodland (Wessington Pasture reserve, owned by the Herefordshire Wildlife Trust) through a gate. Soon turn LEFT and descend through a gate. At the bottom go round to the right and through another gate. Immediately turn RIGHT to a small car park and information board , with a hide and some seats to your

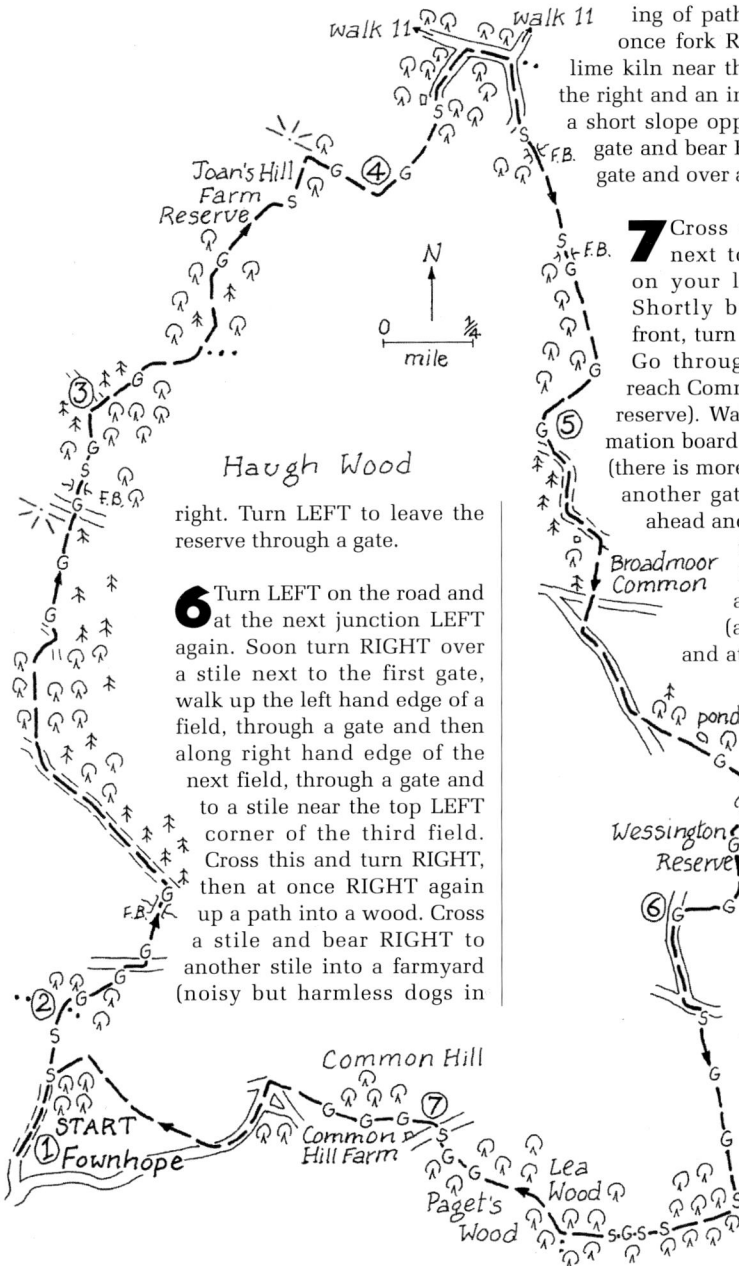

ing of paths turn RIGHT, then at once fork RIGHT. There is an old lime kiln near the end of the wood on the right and an information board down a short slope opposite. Leave through a gate and bear RIGHT through another gate and over a stile to a road.

7 Cross over and keep ahead next to Common Hill Farm on your left. Soon fork LEFT. Shortly before a large gate in front, turn RIGHT through a gate. Go through two more gates to reach Common Hill (another HWT reserve). Walk down past an information board to leave through a gate (there is more of the reserve through another gate to your right), keep ahead and at a junction of tracks take the second on the LEFT. Keep ahead Past an information kiosk (an old telephone box) and at the next junction take the second turning on the RIGHT, past 'Clear View' on your left. Ignore forks to the right. At a cross paths turn LEFT and you will soon find yourself on the grassy track you came up a few hours ago. Buses to Hereford go from the bus stop at the bottom, or you can walk on down to the church and turn RIGHT to find two pubs, the village shop and more bus stops.

Walk 11

Joan's Hill Farm Reserve

N

0 — ¼ mile

Haugh Wood

Broadmoor Common

pond

Wessington Nature Reserve

Common Hill

START
① Fownhope

Common Hill Farm

Paget's Wood

Lea Wood

right. Turn LEFT to leave the reserve through a gate.

6 Turn LEFT on the road and at the next junction LEFT again. Soon turn RIGHT over a stile next to the first gate, walk up the left hand edge of a field, through a gate and then along right hand edge of the next field, through a gate and to a stile near the top LEFT corner of the third field. Cross this and turn RIGHT, then at once RIGHT again up a path into a wood. Cross a stile and bear RIGHT to another stile into a farmyard (noisy but harmless dogs in

2016). Keep ahead to the left of a barn, turn LEFT through a gate and RIGHT over a stile into Lea and Pagets Wood, an HWT reserve of ancient woodland. Keep ahead and at a meet-

DORMINGTON, PENTALOE GLEN & CHECKLEY

DESCRIPTION This 7 mile moderate walk goes through some lovely old woodland and pastures and very varied countryside, with some good views from higher ground. There are a few climbs, the steepest one near the end.

START Bus stop at the turning to Dormington, referred to as 'Dormington, Main Road' in the timetable, SO 583403. If coming by car, park at Swarndon Quarry car park, SO 578386, and see Directions below for how to join the walk.

DIRECTIONS The 476 bus between Hereford and Ledbury stops at Dormington. If coming by car, leave Hereford on the A438 towards Ledbury. About a mile after St Michael's Hospice turn right, signed to Dormington. Take the second turning on the left, signed to Priors Frome and turn right at a T junction. Soon bear left, signed to Woolhope and Checkley. The small car park is on the right just before a sharp bend to the left. From the car park, turn RIGHT on the road, then very soon RIGHT up a track and at once LEFT up a narrow path. Turn RIGHT at a junction through a gate. Now start the walk at section 3, doing sections 1 and 2 at the end.

1 If coming from Hereford, cross over carefully and walk towards the turning signed to Dormington. Cut the corner on the footpath and turn RIGHT. Turn LEFT immediately before the church and walk to the end of this track. Go through a gate and turn RIGHT onto a tarmac lane. Pass a turning on the right after a while and soon, just after 'Lower Hen Hope' on the left and opposite 'Whitgift', climb a small bank on the LEFT to go through a gate.

2 Turn LEFT at a junction. The path ascends for some way, passes a stile on the right, and eventually descends gently to a junction. Turn sharp RIGHT and walk downhill to a road. Turn RIGHT. In about 50 yards, as the road starts to descend more steeply,

fork LEFT on a path. Turn LEFT at a junction through a gate. (If you came by car and started with Section 3, don't turn left; instead walk ahead to return to your car)

3 Walk ahead, enjoying the views to the right. The route goes through another gate, and immediately after this there is a picnic site tucked away 50 yards down the track to your left. If not stopping here, keep ahead from the gate through another one and, later, yet another into a large grassy field. Bear slightly RIGHT through a gate and now keep left downhill. The path enters woodland through a gate and then descends, increasingly steeply, to a track. Turn RIGHT and at the road turn LEFT. (To visit the Moon Inn at Mordiford turn right at the road and in a minute or two the pub is on the right.)

4 Just after Honeysuckle Cottage, at a noticeboard and bench, turn LEFT along the mill leat and soon enter a housing estate. Turn LEFT between numbers 16 and 17 and enter a meadow via a kissing gate. Keep left close to the Pentaloe Brook at first but at a waymark post bear RIGHT across the meadow to bear LEFT on a track. Turn RIGHT just before a bridge to pass a ruined cottage on the left, and leave the meadow by turning LEFT through a gate. Turn LEFT at the next junction. At an open area keep RIGHT uphill.

5 At a little plateau where the track does a sharp turn to the right, bear LEFT through a gap in the far corner on a narrow path into a wood. Cross a stile into a pasture. Head slightly right to leave over another stile at the left hand corner of woodland. The path is not always distinct, but stay quite close to the left hand edge of the wood to reach a track by a bridge. Turn LEFT over the bridge, continue on the track and soon turn RIGHT over a stile. Stay near the stream across two fields and two stiles and through a gate.

6 Just after the gate, turn RIGHT over a footbridge and stile. Keep ahead, bearing slightly left, to cross a stile about 40 yards to the right of the far left hand corner of the field. Cross a footbridge and another stile and then keep to the right hand hedge. When it

A438
to Hereford

① START
Dormington
Church

N

0   ¼
    mile

G ②

Blackbury
Hill

P ③
Alternative
START

to
Mordiford
Inn
④

Pentaloe Brook   G   ⑤

7 Just after passing a cattle grid on your left leading to a drive to Woodbine Cottage, turn LEFT through a gate. Keep straight ahead through three fields and two gates to reach a gated footbridge. Cross this, then keep ahead and go through another gate to reach a path between fences. This leads past a house to a road. Turn RIGHT and almost at once LEFT onto a drive. Go through the left hand gate and, before long, another one. Now keep ahead uphill, ignoring turnings. Join a track coming in from the left and continue uphill until you reach a T junction. Turn sharply RIGHT.

⑧

G Checkley
G G G
F.B.
G

S G S
S S ⑥ S S
F.B.   G
walk 11   ⑦
walk 11

8 When you reach a five-way junction, turn LEFT onto a tarmac road. This climbs quite steeply uphill. Ignore a right turning and before long keep ahead along a grassy track and continue down to the road – take care as the rocky sections can be very slippery. Turn LEFT. Just after Bank Cottage on the left, turn RIGHT down the bridleway you came up at the start of the walk. If you have to wait for the bus, the churchyard at the end of the bridleway makes a pleasant resting place. If you came by car, there is no need to turn right down the bridleway unless you want to see Dormington Church. Instead walk on past the turning and go to the last sentence of Section 1.

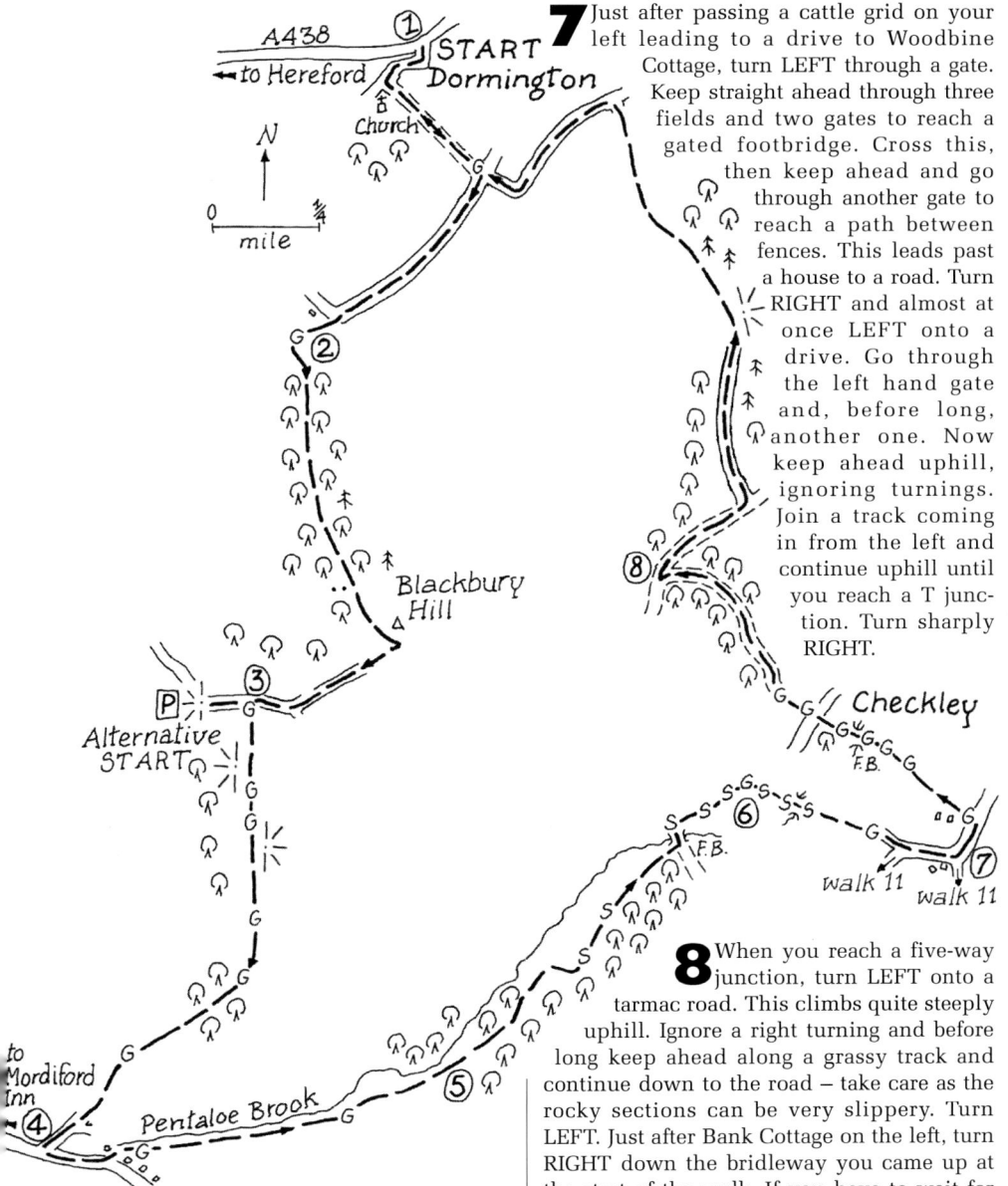

turns right, bear LEFT past a telegraph pole and a fenced ruin just to your right. Pass a stile on the left and go through a gate ahead onto a green lane. Emerge from this onto a road. Keep ahead past a right turn. At the next junction turn LEFT.

WALK 12

WYEVALE WOODS & BREINTON

DESCRIPTION This is an easy 7 mile (6 if coming by car) walk very close to Hereford City. It includes a couple of contrasting woods, one with ancient origins and one recent, a beautiful stretch along the River Wye and some attractive pastures and orchards. Refreshments are available at Wyevale Garden Centre next to the bus stops.
START Bus stops at Wyevale Garden Centre, King's Acre Road, Hereford, SO 471415. Car users should park at the small National Trust car park at Breinton Springs, SO 472396.
DIRECTIONS Several buses stop at Wyevale: the 71/71A/71B between Hereford and Credenhill, the 446 between Hereford and Almeley and the 461/462/463 between Hereford and Kington. For car users, there is a little cul-de-sac lane to the car park about 200 yards west of the turning to Breinton Church. Start the walk at section 5, doing sections 1-4 at the end.

I From the bus stop (coming from Hereford) turn LEFT down the path a few yards further on. In about half a mile, just before a cross tracks, turn LEFT through a gate into a wood. *This is Wyevale Wood, a small reserve owned by Herefordshire Wildlife Trust.* Take any of the paths going through the wood (*if you* ⌐¦⌐ *the middle one, you will pass a memorial stone to Harry and Eileen Williamson, who donated the wood to the Wildlife Trust. Mr Williamson founded Wyevale Garden Centres*) and follow it to the end; then go to the far right hand corner. Here leave through a gate onto a green lane – *a former drovers' route from Wales to Hereford.* Turn LEFT. Just after a pond on the right, turn LEFT and then LEFT again through a gate. *You are now in Drovers Wood, a relatively new wood, acquired by the Woodland Trust in 2000.* Take the LEFT hand path. When you reach a gate at the end

of the wood, do not go through it but follow the path round to the RIGHT and back to the entrance. Leave through the gate you entered by, turn RIGHT and then at once LEFT.

2 Keep ahead until you get to a T junction with a road. Turn RIGHT. Pass a turning on the left and in about 250 yards turn LEFT over a stile. Walk along the left hand side of two fields via another stile. Leave in the corner through a gate onto a path. Soon cross a lane and go through another gate into an orchard. Bear LEFT past a tennis court to yet another gate leading to a road. Cross this and enter another orchard via a fourth gate, bear RIGHT to go through a fifth in a fence about 40 yards from a car park on your right. Turn LEFT to walk round to the right past the lych gate that leads to the church.

3 Turn LEFT at the end of the churchyard and bear RIGHT to a gate. Go through this and walk with sloping woodland to your right and, soon, an orchard to the left. After another gate the path goes along the right hand edge of a field next to a hedge. Just over half way along the field, turn RIGHT through a gate, then LEFT to walk the other side of the hedge. As you approach a house on the left, fork RIGHT down the slope between a large oak tree and a large plane tree (*two of the trees in a 1908 painting, called The Lawns, Warham, by the celebrated Hereford artist Brian Hatton, who was killed in Egypt in 1916; the third tree in the picture has not survived*). Turn RIGHT through a gate and continue to another gate leading to the riverside.

4 On another occasion you could turn left at the river and follow it back into Hereford; this makes a pleasant linear bus walk. Turn RIGHT to follow the river along two large fields and then across a third to a gate onto a track going uphill through the trees. *Before ascending the track you may like to go ahead a little way close to the river to see where Breinton Spring comes out of the rock at the bottom of the bank.* From the gate walk up to a car park.

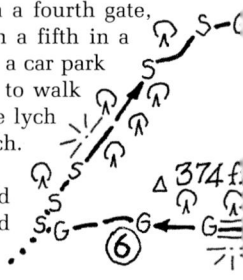

Wyevale Garden Centre

① START

A438

to Hereford

Wyevale Wood

Drover's Wood

②

N

to Hereford

0 ¼ mile

Wye Valley

Upper Breinton

Walk

Breinton

S

Breinton Spring

P ⑤

Breinton Church

③ *Lower Breinton*

Warham House

Alternative Start

River Wye **④**

to Hereford

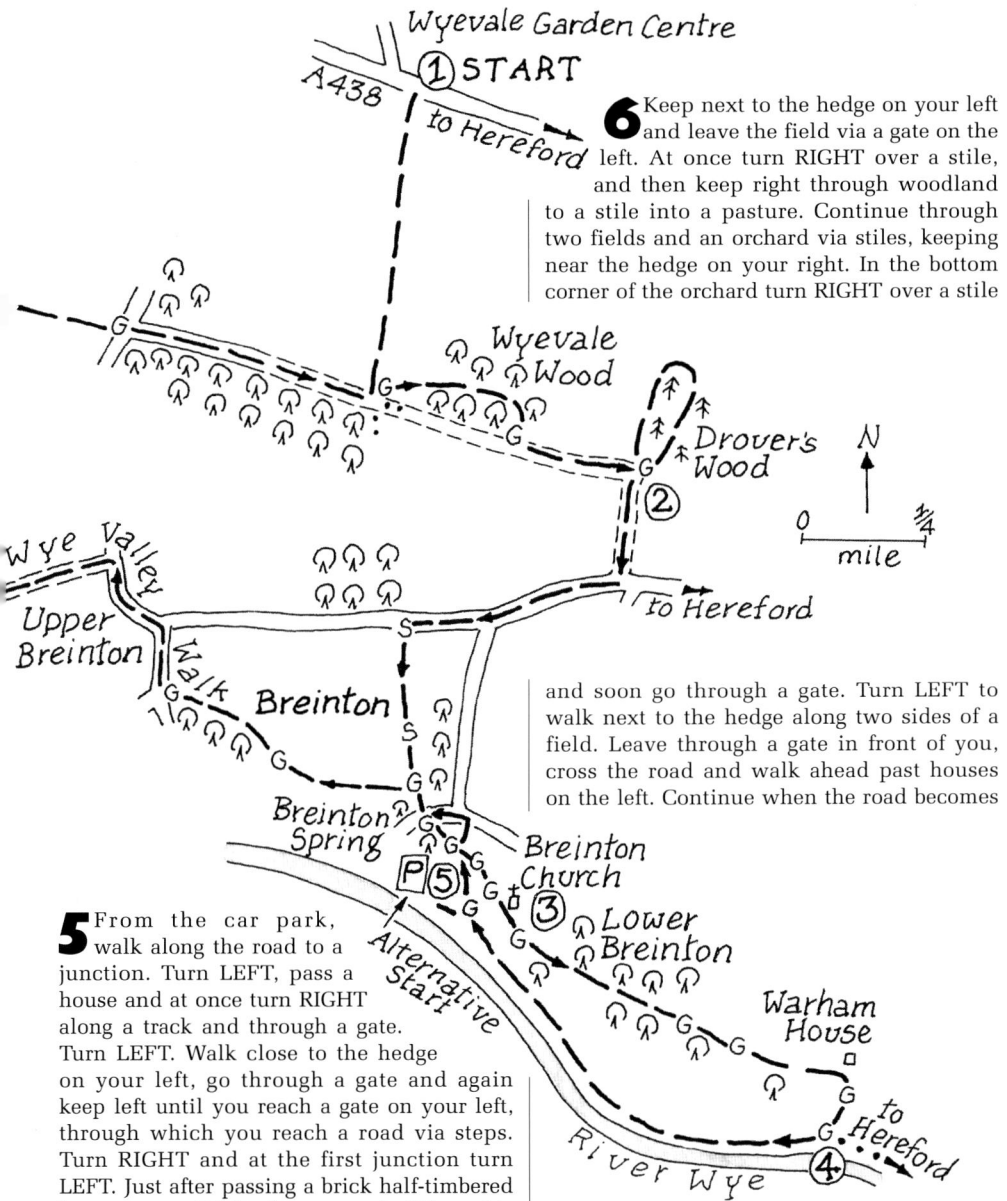

6 Keep next to the hedge on your left and leave the field via a gate on the left. At once turn RIGHT over a stile, and then keep right through woodland to a stile into a pasture. Continue through two fields and an orchard via stiles, keeping near the hedge on your right. In the bottom corner of the orchard turn RIGHT over a stile

and soon go through a gate. Turn LEFT to walk next to the hedge along two sides of a field. Leave through a gate in front of you, cross the road and walk ahead past houses on the left. Continue when the road becomes

5 From the car park, walk along the road to a junction. Turn LEFT, pass a house and at once turn RIGHT along a track and through a gate. Turn LEFT. Walk close to the hedge on your left, go through a gate and again keep left until you reach a gate on your left, through which you reach a road via steps. Turn RIGHT and at the first junction turn LEFT. Just after passing a brick half-timbered house, turn LEFT along a track. When this ends, keep ahead through a gate, straight across a field and through the right hand of two gates. *You're now at the highest point of the walk; there's a trig point (374 feet) off the public footpath a little way up the right hand edge of the field you've just entered.*

a path. At the cross tracks, turn LEFT to return to the bus stops. If you came by car and parked at Breinton Springs, turn RIGHT to enter a wood soon after turning left at the cross tracks; continue at Section 1, ignoring the first two sentences.

WELLINGTON WOOD & WESTHOPE

DESCRIPTION This is an attractive 6 mile walk which starts on an ancient green lane and goes up through Wellington Wood, a large area of sloping ancient woodland. It returns through remote countryside past the 17th C farmhouse of Lawton's Hope. A moderate walk on the whole, but with a long steady climb near the start. Combining this walk with the delightful walk 20 (see Section 3 below) is highly recommended.

START The village shop at Wellington, SO 492482.

DIRECTIONS The 492 bus between Hereford and Leominster goes via Wellington. On some journeys the bus goes through the village, in which case ask for the shop; on other journeys you'll have to alight at Wellington Turn on the A49 and walk along the minor road into the village. If coming by car, park considerately in the village.

1 From the shop, turn LEFT towards the A49. Take the first turning on the LEFT, the cul-de-sac Bridge Lane. When the road ends, keep ahead along, or just above, the old green lane. Cross a minor road and bear LEFT up steps and over a stile. Keep to the right hand edge of the field. Soon after passing a wooden bench, bear RIGHT through a gap in the hedge over a stile and at once keep LEFT along a narrow path. At a tarmac area in front of Hill House, turn RIGHT and follow the track round to the left. The path ascends three sets of steps; after the third of these, bear RIGHT and at once LEFT. You then keep ahead all the way up through the wood, finally emerging through a kissing gate into a wide pasture.

2 Now keep near the right hand fence/hedge, go through a kissing gate ahead and before long pass a cottage on the right.

In about 100 yards bear half LEFT at a waymark post for 30 yards across the corner of a field and continue ahead next to a hedge on your left. Very near the end of the field, turn LEFT through a gate, then turn RIGHT past an old Esso tank. Turn LEFT on a concrete track, then RIGHT in front of a gate. Soon go through a gap. Stay next to the hedge on your left, and look out for a gate in it. Turn LEFT through this, then turn half RIGHT to the far opposite corner. Go through a gate, then along the bottom of the field to another gate; turn LEFT through this. Pass houses on your left and reach a junction with a four way waymark post.

3 If doing walk 20 as well, turn RIGHT here and start walk 20 at section 3, followed by 1 and 2. Turn LEFT and walk downhill to a clearing with a house on your left and an opening just after it. Bear LEFT through this down steps. Cross a track, go through a gate and straight ahead downhill. After crossing a footbridge, turn RIGHT. Go through a gate and then turn half LEFT uphill to go through a gate into a wood. At a junction keep RIGHT near the edge of the wood. Go through one gate, then a second into a farmyard. Turn LEFT and follow the track through old machinery. Soon turn RIGHT to pass a barn on your left. Go through a gate ahead and soon another. Bear RIGHT to continue next to the hedge/fence on your right.

4 Go through a gate into an orchard. Shortly before an old bulldozer in front of you, turn RIGHT through a gate and pass a house on your left. Go down the track, and just after a brick house on your right bear LEFT through a gate into an orchard. Keep ahead and at the end of the orchard return to the track through another gate and continue down to the road. Turn LEFT and in about three quarters of a mile take the next turning on the RIGHT. On reaching a large brick building on the right (an old mill), immediately turn LEFT down a narrow path (easy to miss) to walk near the stream on your right. After a gate, a field, a stile, another field, another stile and a path, you reach Bridge Lane. Turn RIGHT back to the start.

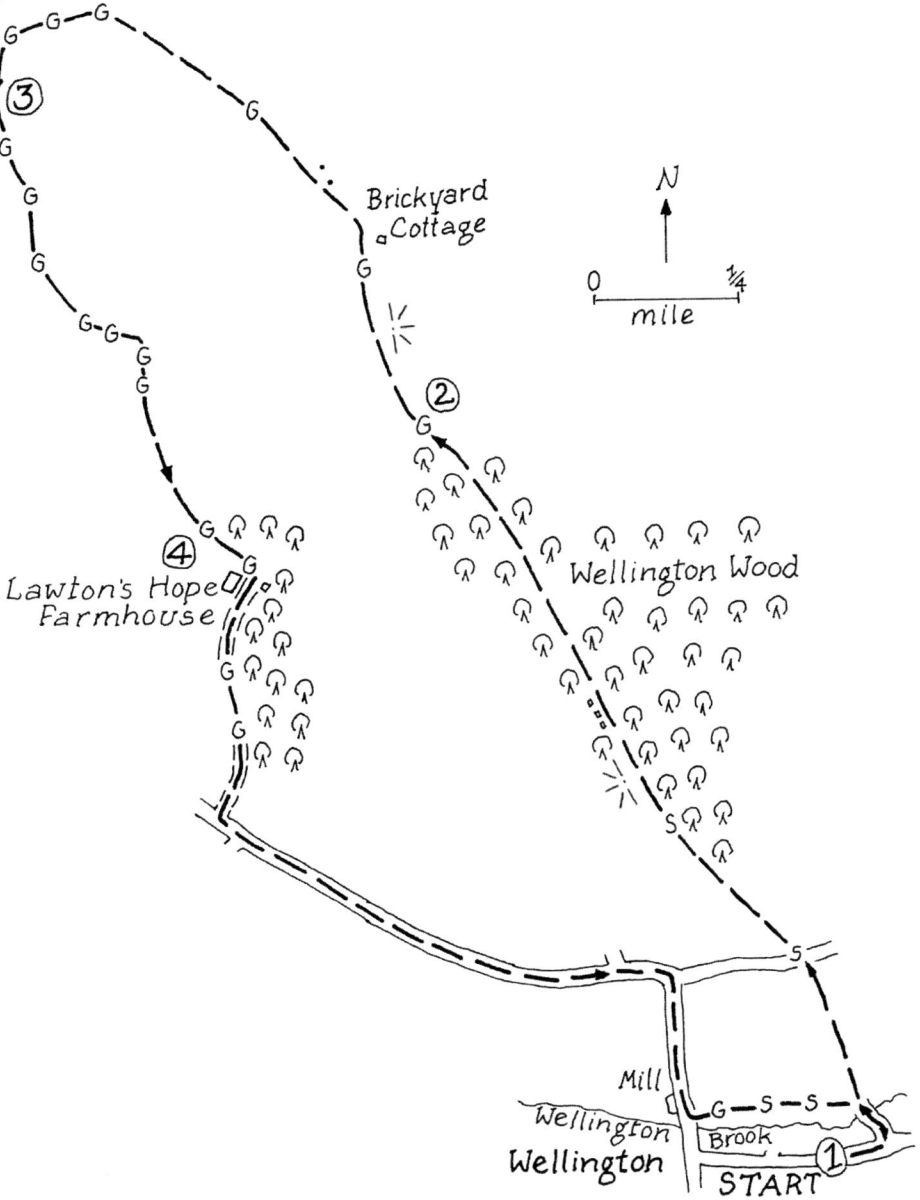

Westhope

Walk 20

③

G—G—G

G

G

G

G

G—G

G

G

Brickyard
Cottage

G

②
G

Wellington Wood

④
G
Lawton's Hope
Farmhouse

G

G

S

S

S

Mill
Wellington Brook
Wellington

G—S—S

①
START

N

0   ¼
mile

27

WALK 14
QUEENSWOOD & BODENHAM LAKE

DESCRIPTION This is a moderate 6 mile (8 with the optional extension) walk between two beautiful nature reserves, both of which are now managed by the Herefordshire Wildlife Trust and New Leaf. (Walks through the very popular Queenswood arboretum and reserve are described on a leaflet available from the shop there.) This walk takes a delightful circular route to Bodenham Lake, a nature reserve created from former gravel pits, which is less well known but well worth a visit, with its orchards and lakeside setting, including a bird hide. There is a short optional extension, which goes along the river, on a quiet road and back through a little wood.

START Queenswood bus stops, SO 507515.

DIRECTIONS The 492 bus between Hereford and Leominster stops at Queenswood. If coming by car, there is a large car park next to the Visitor Centre (clearly signed from the A49).

1 From the Visitor Centre or bus stop (if coming from Hereford) cross the A49 carefully, using the refuge in the centre of the road. Turn LEFT and walk along the grass verge. In about 100 yards, opposite a drive on the other side of the road, turn RIGHT through a gate onto a path. Turn RIGHT when you get to a T junction and stay on the stony track, which leaves the wood and before long goes through a gate by a cattle grid, and then past a farmhouse.

2 As the track bends to the left over a cattle grid, leave it by continuing ahead over the grass and through a gate. Keep ahead through another gate and then along the right hand edge of a field. Shortly after the next gate, the path forks RIGHT away from the field and quite soon reaches a gate leading to a grassy plateau. Bear RIGHT here and go down to the far corner of the meadow. Leave

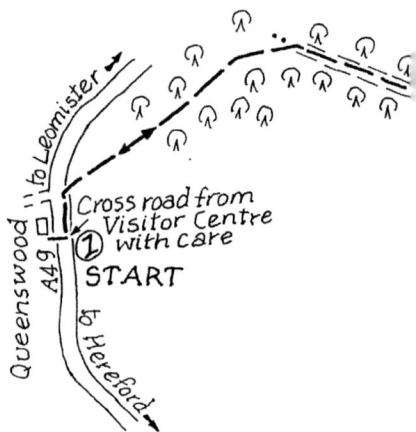

through a gate onto a track. Follow this to join a drive down to the road.

3 Turn LEFT and in about 60 yards turn RIGHT through a gate to walk next to a hedge on your left. After two more gates bear slightly RIGHT through a gap in the hedge and straight on to enter the churchyard through a gate. (*The church has some interesting medieval features.*) Walk past the lych gate and the church entrance and leave the churchyard through the gate in the far left hand corner. Cross a small bridge. If you want to do the extension to the walk, continue with Section 4; if not, turn RIGHT at once through a gate/turnstile and go to Section 6.

4 Continue in the same direction to cross a larger bridge over the River Lugg. Turn RIGHT to follow the river bank to the end of the field. Cross a stiled footbridge and go straight across the next field to cross another footbridge. Bear RIGHT up a short slope, cross a double stile and walk up into a field. Head half RIGHT across the field to go through a gap in the hedge and on through a gate onto a drive. Turn LEFT on the road, which bends right and then left. In about half a mile, you reach a T junction.

5 Turn LEFT here. Just after the turning to Litmarsh on your right, turn LEFT through a gate on a drive. Soon after the drive bends right, turn LEFT over a stile and keep next to the fence on your left. When you reach a second field, turn RIGHT uphill next to a hedge to your right. At the top, the path enters woodland and before long

lake.. Turn LEFT through a gate and continue through another gate to reach a car park. Turn LEFT and walk along a wide path. When you reach fencing on the left (*this used to be a sailing centre, but its use is currently under discussion*) turn RIGHT with the track. Go through a gate and turn LEFT.

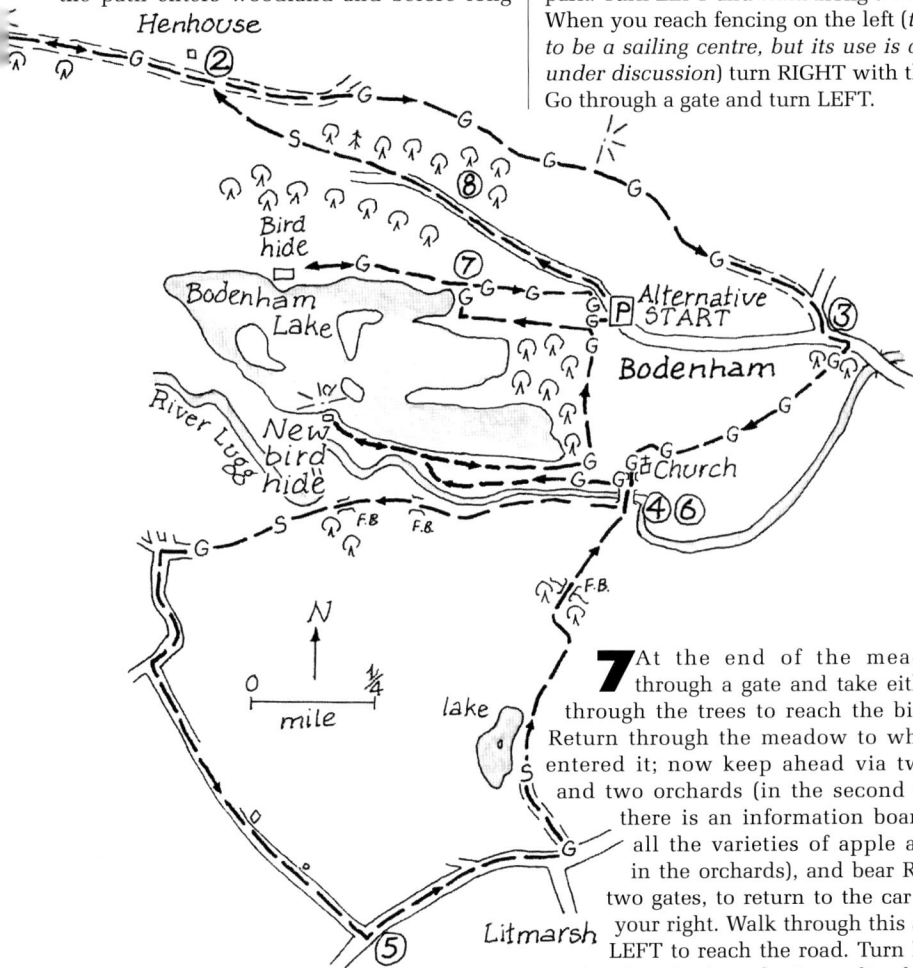

Henhouse

Bird hide

Bodenham Lake

River Lugg

New bird hide

F.B.   F.B.

Alternative **P** START

Bodenham

Church

F.B.

N

0   ¼
mile

lake

7 At the end of the meadow go through a gate and take either path through the trees to reach the bird hide. Return through the meadow to where you entered it; now keep ahead via two gates and two orchards (in the second of these there is an information board about all the varieties of apple and pear in the orchards), and bear RIGHT to two gates, to return to the car park on your right. Walk through this and turn LEFT to reach the road. Turn LEFT. In a few hundred yards, immediately after a drive on the right, fork RIGHT up a narrow path into woodland.

Litmarsh

descends steeply down steps. Cross a gated footbridge and walk straight across the meadow towards the church. Cross the River Lugg and turn LEFT through a gate/turnstile.

6 Walk along a muddy path with the river on the left. Enter the reserve through a gate onto a large grassy area. Walk ahead for a view of the river on your left, then bear RIGHT towards the lake. Go through a gate ahead and walk along a path to reach the new (2017) bird hide overlooking the lake. Then return along the grass close to the

8 At a T junction turn LEFT, then soon RIGHT up steps. Leave the wood over a stile and bear LEFT to walk to the left of an enclosed copse, then to the right of another. This takes you back to the track you came on earlier, so bear LEFT to return to the wood. As the track begins to descend, some way into the wood, fork LEFT onto a grassy path to return to the start.

WALK 15

WEOBLEY, BURTON HILL & GARNSTONE PARK

DESCRIPTION This 6 mile moderate walk starts at Weobley, one of the most attractive and well known Black and White villages in Herefordshire. The walk is over flat farmland and parkland at the beginning and end respectively, but in the middle there is a very steep (hence the overall classification as moderate) climb up through beautiful woodland. Before or after the walk you may like to follow the interesting Jubilee Heritage Trail around Weobley village; descriptive leaflets are available from the shop, and information plaques are placed throughout the village. Refreshments are available in Weobley at the Green Bean Café, Jules Café/Restaurant and at Ye Olde Salutation Inn.

START Bus stop at Broad Street, Weobley, in the centre of the village, SO 403516.

DIRECTIONS The 461/462/463 bus between Hereford and Kington stops in the centre of Weobley. If coming by car, drive downhill from the bus stops towards the church and turn LEFT at the Red Lion (now an Indian Restaurant) to find a car park a short way along on the right, SO 401517.

1 From the bus stop in Broad Street walk uphill and turn RIGHT at Ye Olde Salutation Inn, then RIGHT again at the T junction. Turn LEFT next to the first house (Marlbrook House), go through the gate and follow the track uphill and into a field. At the top go through a kissing gate and keep straight ahead to go through a second kissing gate and soon a third. Turn RIGHT to walk next to the hedge. When you reach a stile on the right, turn LEFT straight across the field. Go through, in turn, a gate, a field, and two more gates to reach a small meadow. Then cross a stile and walk past the house on the left. *This is The Ley, a remarkable timber-framed house, very little altered externally since it was built in about 1589.*

2 Soon pass a green with an old cider press. Turn LEFT, then RIGHT on a concrete track. Ignore turnings off this. When the concrete ends, keep ahead along the grass next to the hedge. Go through a gate, then a footbridge. Bear slightly RIGHT across the field and then continue on a grassy track with a hedge to your left at first. At a T junction of tracks, turn RIGHT and follow the track round to the left and on until it ends at a field in front of you. Turn LEFT with the hedge on your left and walk round two sides of the field; then go through a gap into the next field. Turn LEFT at the end of this field to walk uphill with the hedge on your right. Leave the field onto a road.

3 Turn LEFT and walk with care for a short distance along this road. Soon after a drive (signed Private Road) on the right, turn RIGHT up a shady path which soon joins the drive. Walk up this past houses and through two gates by cattle grids. When the tarmac ends, continue straight ahead on a path through a gate. On reaching a forestry track, turn LEFT and follow the track round to the right. Look for, and take, a waymarked narrow path on the RIGHT cutting a corner to reach another forestry track. (If you miss it, you will soon reach the second forestry track on your right.) Cross this and continue steeply uphill. At a T junction with a wider track, keep ahead onto it, soon passing a trig point (Burton Hill, 287 m) on your left.

4 At the end of the grassy track you reach a junction. Take care here as your path is easily missed. There is a wide track going downhill to your left. Do not take this but instead turn sharp LEFT down a narrow grassy path to the left of the wide track. Turn RIGHT at the bottom. Leave the wood through a gate and descend on the track, which after a while bends round to the left. Cross a stile and when the track turns right, turn LEFT to go through a gate ahead. Turn half RIGHT towards the left hand end of a wall and go through a gate onto a track. Turn RIGHT.

5 Go through a gate and, on reaching a fence in front, turn LEFT, soon going through a gate. Now maintain the same direction, towards the church in the distance, through a field, over a track, through another field and through a gate. Then keep ahead; the path bends slightly to the right past an oak tree to another gate. Once through this, walk straight on through the old earthworks of Weobley Castle; there is an information board about this at the end, just before a final gate brings you back to the start.

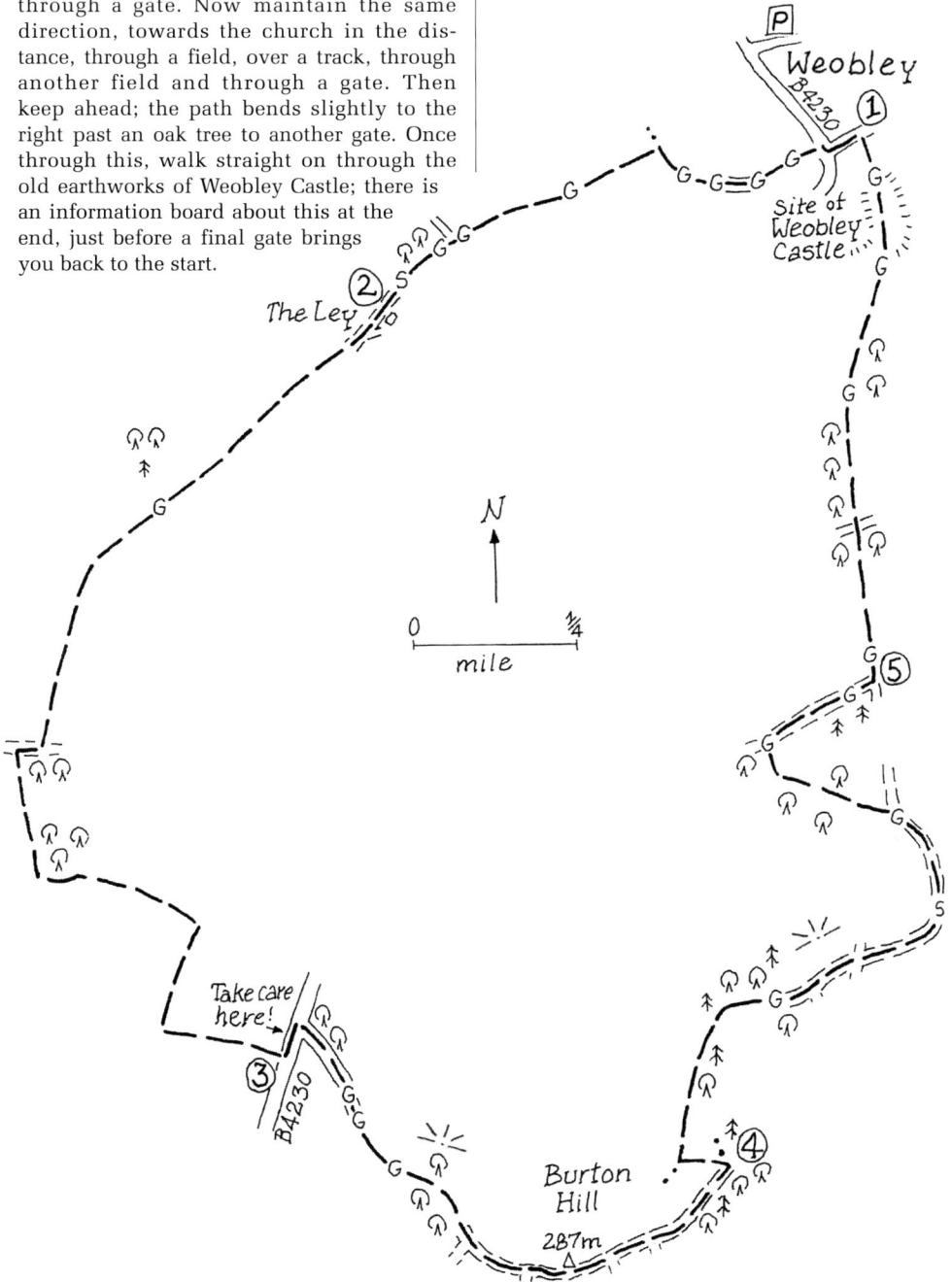

P

Weobley

B4230

①

Site of
Weobley
Castle

The Ley

②

N

0 ¼
mile

⑤

⑤

Take care
here!

③

B4230

④

Burton
Hill

287m

STOKE PRIOR & RISBURY

DESCRIPTION This 10 mile moderate walk has a bit of everything – woods, streams, hills, orchards, pastureland, farmland, a pretty village, a green burial ground and a car dismantlers' yard.

START Leominster Railway Station, SO 502589.

DIRECTIONS There are frequent trains to Leominster from Hereford and Shrewsbury. If coming by car there are long stay car parks in Broad Street and Dishley Street, both within walking distance of the station.

I Walk down the access road from the station and turn RIGHT at the end. As the road bends left, turn RIGHT again down a path taking you to a bridge over the station and then another bridge over the river. Turn RIGHT down steps on a path which stays close to the river for nearly half a mile and then turns left in front of a stile ahead. Quite soon cross another stile ahead to reach the road. Keep ahead and in about 90 yards turn LEFT through a gate to walk uphill on a wide grassy path. Bear LEFT up steps and at the next junction turn RIGHT downhill. Before long bear LEFT uphill again, soon going up steps into woodland. Cross a track by an entrance to Widgeon Wood on your left and continue uphill to reach a stile.

2 Cross this and turn RIGHT. Turn RIGHT through the next gate, then at once LEFT. Now keep ahead through a field, a gate and another field. Then cross a bridge and bear slightly LEFT towards a gap in the hedge opposite. Go through this and turn LEFT, then soon RIGHT off the track (no waymark in 2016) with a hedge to your left. Cross a stile, then later another, and cut the corner of a field to cross a third stile. Now cross the field to go through a gate in the middle of the hedge. Walk down to a stile taking you to a road. Turn LEFT, then RIGHT at the cross-roads. Just after The Wain House and before a bridge, turn LEFT over a stile.

3 Walk uphill towards the far corner of the vast meadow and when you reach it turn RIGHT downhill to cross a stile ahead into a wood. Follow the path down the left hand side of the wood, leave through a gate and cross an old bridge. Then turn LEFT and keep close to the stream. When you reach a large door in front, cross a stile just to its left, and continue between stacks of written off cars, keeping left. Look carefully for a gap between cars leading to steps on the RIGHT and turn up them. Bear RIGHT up a drive and cross a stile to leave the yard; then bear RIGHT again up a grassy slope to cross another stile. Cross the field to where the hedge in front ends at a gap at its right hand end. Go through this and stay next to the hedge on your right to reach a stile leading to a road.

4 Cross with care and enter another field just to your left. Walk ahead to the left of a hedge down three fields; in the third one, when the hedge turns right, keep ahead to a gate leading to a road. Turn RIGHT and then LEFT at the cross-roads. Turn LEFT at the next cross-roads and in about 200 yards turn RIGHT over a stile. The public footpath goes straight ahead, but you can look around if you wish. Walk straight ahead through the woodland and on across the next field to cross a stile. Turn LEFT and follow the edge of the field round to the right; soon bear LEFT down a path and over a footbridge on the LEFT into woodland.

5 There is a clear path through this; leave through a gate ahead and turn LEFT. Soon turn RIGHT over a footbridge into a field. Go half LEFT across this and through a gate. Turn RIGHT to walk past a ruined building and on downhill. At the bottom go through a gate and over a footbridge into more woodland. Quite soon leave over a stile and walk along a grassy path with the steep slope of Risbury hillfort (*not accessible*) to your left. Walk close to the stream as far as a gated footbridge; turn RIGHT over this, then LEFT to walk next to the stream through an orchard. At the end of this turn RIGHT through a gate to reach a road. Turn RIGHT.

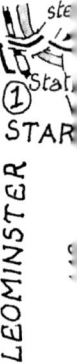

6 In a few hundred yards turn LEFT along a drive signed to Hollyw4ll Farm. Shortly before reaching the farm turn RIGHT

8 Cross over and walk ahead, passing The Lamb Inn on the left. In a few hundred yards turn RIGHT through a waymarked gate, into an orchard. Soon cross a stile and at the top another. Turn LEFT and keep left into woodland. Continue in the same direction, later forking LEFT down to enter woodland in front. Turn LEFT here and go over two stiles to reach a road. Turn RIGHT, and LEFT at the next drive. As the drive divides,

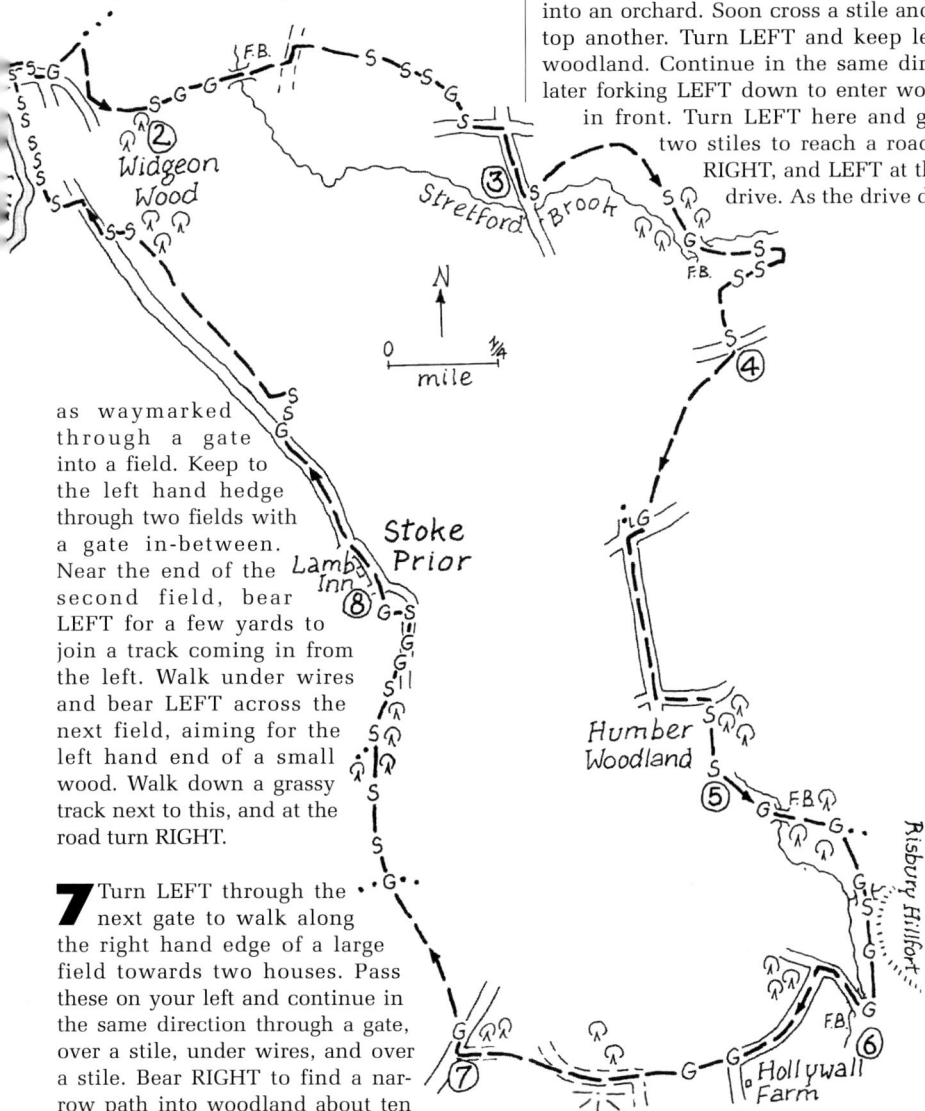

Widgeon Wood

Stretford Brook

F.B.

N

0   ¼
mile

Stoke Prior

Lamb Inn

Humber Woodland

Risbury Hillfort

Hollywall Farm

as waymarked through a gate into a field. Keep to the left hand hedge through two fields with a gate in-between. Near the end of the second field, bear LEFT for a few yards to join a track coming in from the left. Walk under wires and bear LEFT across the next field, aiming for the left hand end of a small wood. Walk down a grassy track next to this, and at the road turn RIGHT.

7 Turn LEFT through the next gate to walk along the right hand edge of a large field towards two houses. Pass these on your left and continue in the same direction through a gate, over a stile, under wires, and over a stile. Bear RIGHT to find a narrow path into woodland about ten yards from the right hand fence. Soon cross a stile. Leave over another stile and join a track through a gate, then another. Keep ahead and as the track bends right, turn LEFT into a pasture. Soon turn RIGHT through a gate. Pass between houses and bear LEFT down a path to a road.

turn RIGHT over a stile and keep left, soon with the river on your left. After five stiles you reach a road. Cross this and the stile ahead to join the route you came out on. Don't forget to turn LEFT over two bridges to return to the station.

KIMBOLTON, STOCKTON RIDE & EATON HILL

DESCRIPTION This 8 mile moderate walk starts on the flat farmland typical of much of the countryside round Leominster, but soon leaves this to visit the village of Kimbolton and to go to its hilltop church via the wooded green lane of Stockton Ride – formerly used by wealthy local landowners. The walk then takes a varied undulating route back, including a section along Eaton Hill high above Leominster with good views of the town and beyond.

START Leominster Railway Station, SO 502589.

DIRECTIONS There are frequent trains to Leominster from Hereford and Shrewsbury. If coming by car there are long stay car parks in Broad Street and Dishley Street, within walking distance of the station; car users may prefer to make their way to the Priory church and start the walk from the churchyard, in the middle of Section 1 below.

1 Walk down from the station to the road. Turn RIGHT. Where the road bends left, keep ahead along Pinsley Road as it winds its way (turn LEFT at a post box and RIGHT at a wall in front of you) to a green with a large building (Grange Court) on your left. Turn half-RIGHT on a path under the trees, and soon (with the war memorial to your left) bear slightly RIGHT again through wooden gates towards the church. Leave the churchyard in the far left hand corner down a few steps, cross over and walk down the street called, rather confusingly, 'The Priory'. Go straight ahead over an iron bridge and turn RIGHT. When you get to a road, turn RIGHT and walk over a level crossing to a roundabout. Cross the busy road with great care and keep ahead, walking towards Ludlow.

2 Immediately after a right turn (Hay Lane) bear RIGHT over a stile; then keep RIGHT through woodland and along the edge of a large field. At the end of this, turn RIGHT over a stile and bridge, then LEFT next to the brook. Keep close to this along a field, over two stiles embedded in gates and then keep to the left along another field. At the end of this, cross a stile to a road, cross this and another stile and again stay close to the brook. Cross a stile and when you reach a house in front of you, turn LEFT over a gated footbridge and soon cross a double stile on the right to reach a lane.

3 Turn LEFT up this and walk straight up to a junction. Turn LEFT. Turn RIGHT immediately after the Stockton Cross Inn (*good for refreshments*), then at once LEFT along a shady sunken lane, Stockton Ride, an old green lane. Ignore a left fork, and when you reach a stile leading into a field (no waymark in 2017), turn RIGHT over it. If you look half-left, you will now see a large green barn two fields away. Walk down the field to cross another stile and keep ahead to cross, in turn, a field, a stile, another field and another stile to reach a road junction.

4 Cross over and walk ahead; at the next junction turn RIGHT through a gate leading to 'Ashfield' and straight ahead through another gate into a pasture. Walk on past a lone oak tree to cross a stile, a field and another stile. Then turn LEFT along the edge of the field to leave it via a stile at the bottom taking you to a footbridge and a gate into another field. Walk up the field towards the church; in the top corner cross a stile, then soon another to reach a road, on the other side of which a footpath leads you into the churchyard.

5 Walk straight ahead if not visiting the church to leave through a gate. Bear LEFT to a kissing gate leading to a road. Turn RIGHT. At the junction, cross the main road with care and take the right hand lane (signed to Grantsfield). At the T junction cross the road ahead, and then cross a stile slightly to your right. Bear RIGHT uphill towards a Dutch barn. Leave the field through a gate, cross the road and continue on the track to the right of

the Dutch barn. Cross a brook and go straight ahead upwards to go through a gate into an orchard. Turn RIGHT and follow the track round to the left and on through the orchard, leaving through a gate ahead. Turn RIGHT into woodland.

6 At the end of the wood, cross a stile to a road and turn LEFT, then RIGHT over another stile. Walk downhill next to the fence on the right, soon entering trees again. On emerging from these, bear slightly LEFT down to the bottom of the slope to where a track comes in from the left. Turn RIGHT on this over a bridge, then LEFT along the right hand edge of a field. Walk diagonally LEFT up the next field, turn LEFT through a gate, then RIGHT with the hedge on your right. Cross a stile and go downhill until you reach a junction with a green track.

7 Turn RIGHT. Cross a stile and soon stay next to the left hand edge of a field. Cross a stile into woodland and later another, walking

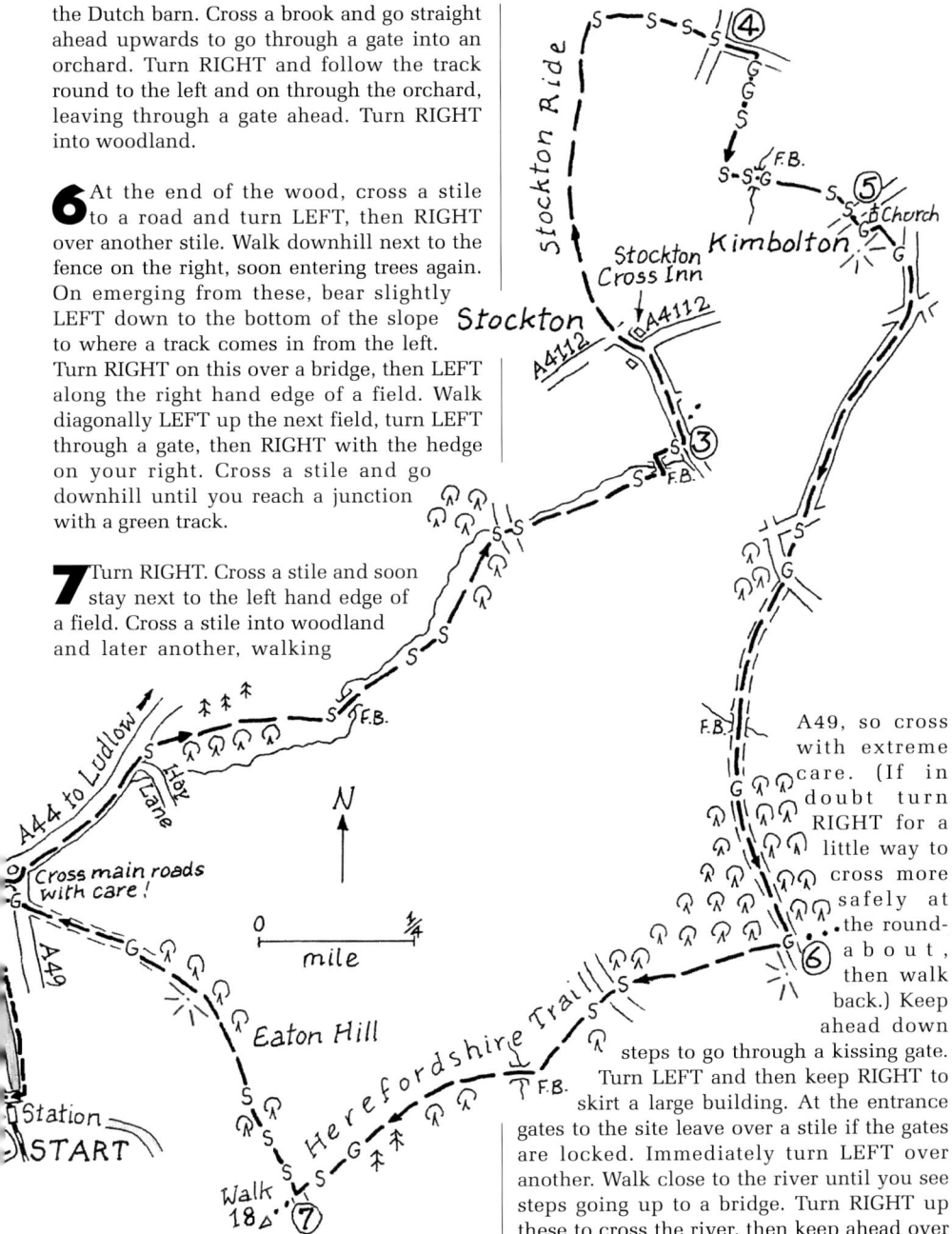

A49, so cross with extreme care. (If in doubt turn RIGHT for a little way to cross more safely at the roundabout, then walk back.) Keep ahead down steps to go through a kissing gate. Turn LEFT and then keep RIGHT to skirt a large building. At the entrance gates to the site leave over a stile if the gates are locked. Immediately turn LEFT over another. Walk close to the river until you see steps going up to a bridge. Turn RIGHT up these to cross the river, then keep ahead over another bridge crossing the railway. Walk along the path to the road. Turn LEFT, then LEFT again to return to the station.

along near the top of Eaton Hill. Join a track, which goes through a gate and then gently downhill to the road. This is the very busy

Map labels:

Stockton Ride

Stockton Cross Inn

Kimbolton

Church

Stockton

A4112

A44 to Ludlow

Hoi Lane

A49

Cross main roads with care!

N

0 — ¼ mile

Eaton Hill

Herefordshire Trail

Station START

Walk 18

F.B.

WALK 18

BACHE CAMP

DESCRIPTION This 9 mile moderate walk leaves Leominster to go through peaceful farmland next to the Whittey Brook, and then climbs gradually to reach Bache Camp, one of the most remarkable of Herefordshire's hill forts because of its remote and dramatic setting which can be seen from some distance away. The walk returns through attractive countryside along part of the Herefordshire Trail.
START Leominster Railway Station, SO 502589.
DIRECTIONS Same as for walk 17.

1 & 2 These are the same as Sections 1 and 2 of walk 18.

3 Turn RIGHT and at once LEFT through a gate (towards Brook House Farm). Follow the drive to the left of the house, then across an open area with a garage to your left. Leave over a stile ahead. Again keep close to the brook on your left; the route crosses a field, a stile, a road, a stile and a field, then goes through a kissing gate into an orchard. After a gate, a field and another gate walk along the drive of a house on your left. When the drive bends right, keep ahead through a gate and bear slightly RIGHT to cross a stile on the other side of the field. Keep left in the next field and leave through a gate ahead. Turn RIGHT and at once LEFT on a road. After a while pass, on the right, a stile and, a little later, the entrance to Bachefield House.

4 A few minutes later turn RIGHT up steps and over a stile. Walk up the field to the top LEFT corner. Cross another stile and now keep the fence/hedge on your left; at the end of this field turn LEFT over a stile. Then turn half-RIGHT down to go through a gate/stile in the far corner. Now walk downhill, keeping quite close to the hedge on your right, with a good view of Bache Camp ahead to your right. At the valley bottom, go through a gate, over a footbridge and through another gate. Then keep ahead uphill to

a gate leading to a road; don't go through this but turn RIGHT towards a gate about 50 yards from the field corner. Go through this and at the end of the field turn RIGHT through another gate. Turn LEFT here into the camp if you want to wander around it to get an idea of its size and splendid position.

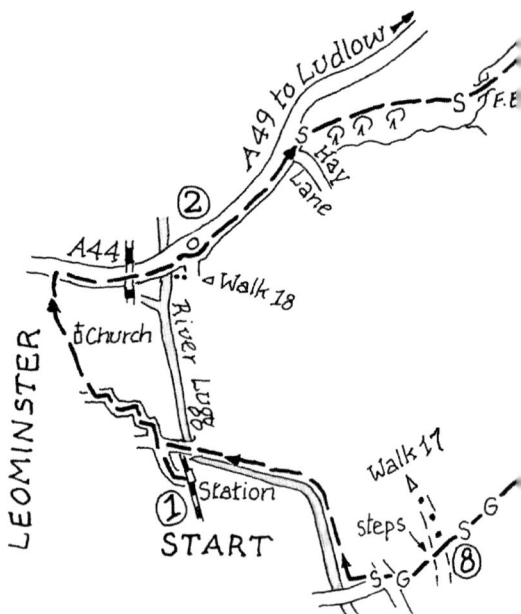

5 From the gate where you entered the camp, walk ahead downhill to cross a gated footbridge. Turn LEFT. Follow the winding track up to, and through, a farm. Continue, soon going round to the right by a barn. When the track becomes a tarmac lane, turn LEFT over a stile. Keep to the right along the edge of the field and cross a stile at its end. Turn RIGHT, then in a few yards LEFT to walk downhill, before long next to a hedge, then a barn, on your left. Turn LEFT over a stile, then RIGHT down a short drive to a road.

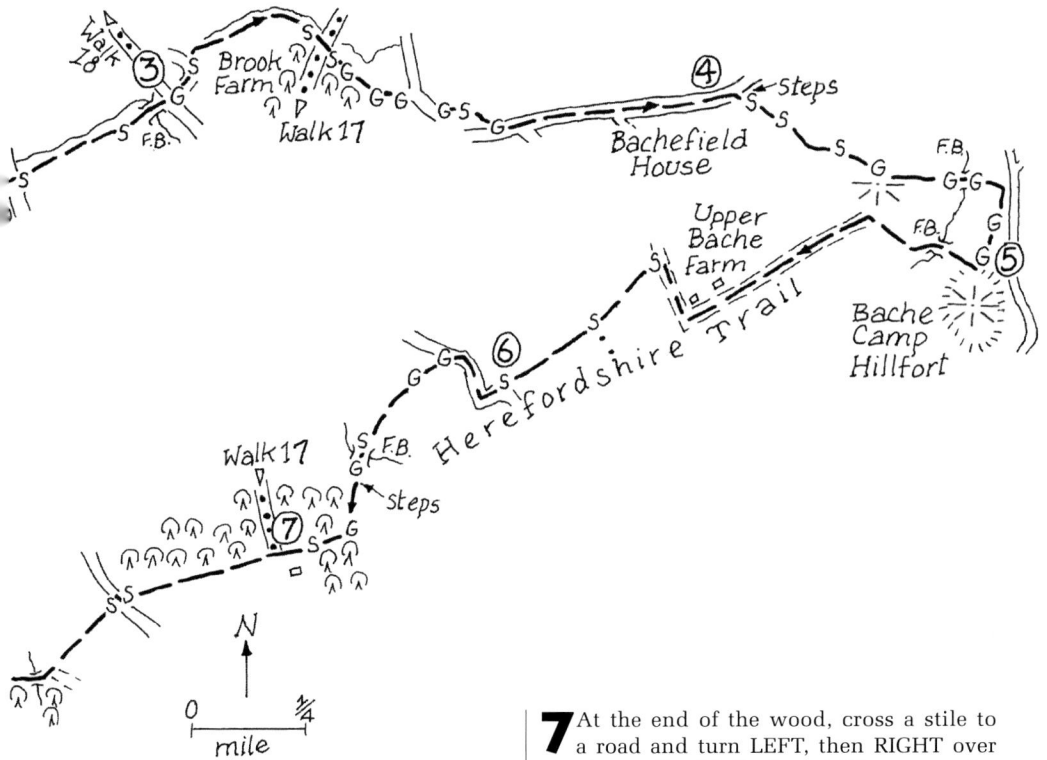

Brook Farm

Walk 17

Bachefield House

Steps

Upper Bache Farm

Bache Camp Hillfort

Herefordshire Trail

Walk 17

F.B.

steps

N

0   ¼
          mile

6 Turn RIGHT. Just after a large house and stable on the left, and opposite a track on the right, turn LEFT through a gate, then before long go through another and round to the RIGHT through a gateway. Turn LEFT. At the end of the field cross a stile to a footbridge. Go through a gate and up a few steps, then walk up to the far LEFT hand corner of the field. Go through a gate into an orchard and go very slightly to the left to walk ahead next to a hedge on your right. Before long cross another stile and continue, with a house to your left. Once past this, your path ahead enters woodland.

7 At the end of the wood, cross a stile to a road and turn LEFT, then RIGHT over another stile. Walk downhill next to the fence on the right, soon entering trees again. On emerging from these, bear slightly LEFT down to the bottom of the slope to where a track comes in from the left. Turn RIGHT on this over a bridge, then soon LEFT to walk along the right hand edge of a field. Walk diagonally LEFT up the next field, turn LEFT through a gate, then RIGHT with the hedge on your right. Cross a stile and go downhill until you reach a junction with a green track.

8 Cross the track to go down steps; then continue down a wide green sward to go through a gate to a road. Turn RIGHT. Just after passing West Eaton (care home), cross a stile on your RIGHT. Follow the path as it turns right in front of the river and continue on it keeping as close to the river as you can. Go under a road bridge and soon up steps. Turn LEFT on a footbridge over the river and then cross another bridge over the railway. Walk down the path to the road. Turn LEFT and soon LEFT again to return to the station.

WALK 19

FISHPOOL VALLEY & CROFT AMBREY

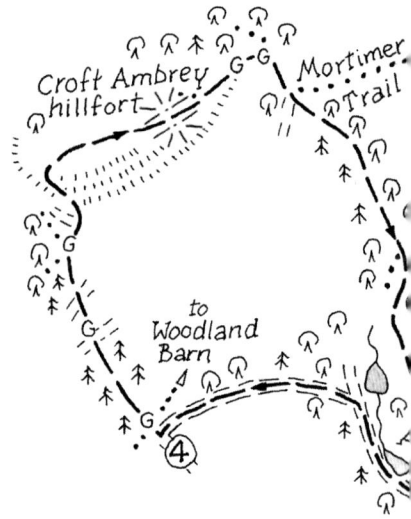

DESCRIPTION This is a superb moderate 7 (5½ if coming by car) mile walk, which starts in the pretty village of Yarpole and goes through the beautiful wooded Fishpool Valley of the Croft Castle estate, to reach Croft Ambrey Iron Age hill fort with spectacular ramparts and views. It returns via woodland, common land and countryside. (There are other excellent walks on the Croft estate waymarked with different colours by the National Trust, but to use any of these in full you should either be a member of the National Trust or pay for entry to the grounds.)

START Bircher Turn (where the B 4362 meets a minor road from Gorbett Bank) if coming by bus, SO 478653. If coming by car, park near Yarpole church, SO 470648, and omit section 1 below.

DIRECTIONS The 490 bus between Leominster and Ludlow calls at Bircher Turn (the stop after Gorbett Bank if coming from Leominster).

1 Walk with great care on the left-hand side of the road (to avoid having to cross twice) as signed towards Croft Castle. After about 120 yards turn LEFT over a stile into a camp site. Keep straight ahead via a gate/stile, then bear slightly RIGHT to pass a magnificent oak tree. Leave over a stile and walk ahead through two fields via a gate. Pass an old stile and then keep next to the hedge on the left. After another gate keep right and at the end of the field go through a gate to a road. Turn LEFT, then soon RIGHT to walk into Yarpole.

2 Turn RIGHT at the next junction (signed towards Cockgate) and walk past the church, with its remarkable detached bell tower, and containing an excellent community shop and café. Later pass the Bell Inn. Soon after passing Ivy Dene on your right (a brick house with railings) turn LEFT down the drive of The Old School House. Pass the house via a gate on its right and go through a small patch of garden to leave over a stile. Keep to the right hand edge of the field and at the end turn RIGHT through a gate and, soon, another leading to a road. Cross with care and go through a gate into parkland. Keep ahead across a field and a stile and then bear slightly LEFT to a stile leading to a road (the drive to Croft Castle).

3 Turn LEFT. In about 100 yards bear RIGHT down a track. Continue down this for some way, ignoring turnings and passing fish pools and an old 'Gothic' pump house on the right (with some of the old machinery still visible inside). A few minutes after this you will reach a multiple junction with a lime kiln, a quarry and a noticeboard to your left. Turn LEFT here (not sharp left) and walk past the old quarry and lime kiln to your right. Ignore a left fork and continue uphill. Another path comes in from the right; immediately after this keep ahead, still uphill. At the top the route turns left but you may like to divert by turning RIGHT, going through a gate and on for a minute or two to reach the Wood Pasture Barn, with information about the ancient trees around you.

38

4 Turn LEFT, then soon RIGHT through a gate. Cross another track and go through another gate. In another minute or two fork RIGHT through a gate. Continue to the right and soon turn LEFT. Keep LEFT at a junction and follow the path as it bends round to the right and on through the hill fort, with spectacular views on a good day. At a junction

(where the National Trust blue trail turns right) keep ahead. Go through a gate and turn RIGHT and take the next turning on the RIGHT through another gate (Mortimer Trail sign). At the next junction turn RIGHT, then immediately LEFT down a narrower path. Near the bottom pass two paths to the right and take the next turning on the RIGHT.

5 Just after Highwood Bank Quarry and noticeboard on the left, ignore a right fork down steps and keep ahead. Leave the wood through a kissing gate and go ahead slightly to your left to walk along the lower edge of the common. You will pass several grassy tracks to your right. By about the ninth of these, you should find that it goes towards some houses. Turn RIGHT down this track, which joins a stony track coming in from the right, passes Neal Cottage and The White House and finally crosses a cattle grid to

become a tarmac road. (If you turn down from the common too soon, just turn LEFT at the bottom and walk on until you pass Neal Cottage.) Soon after Byecroft on the left, as the road bends left, turn RIGHT through a gate.

6 Keep near the hedge on the left, go through a gate, and continue next to the hedge. Go past a large gap in the hedge to a gate leading to a road. Cross this, go through a gate slightly to your left and cross a field, bearing slightly LEFT to go through another gate. Turn RIGHT and keep next to the edge of the field. Well before the corner, turn RIGHT through a gate, then turn LEFT and walk near the left hand side of the sloping field, At the end go through a gate about 40 yards down from the left hand corner. Keep right through the next two fields, going through two more gates, eventually reaching a road.

7 Turn LEFT here if going back to catch a bus, or turn RIGHT to return to the village and the church if you parked there. To return to the junction where the bus stops, turn LEFT again at the next junction, then RIGHT through the gate you came through earlier. Continue through fields and the campsite to reach a road, then turn RIGHT back to where the walk started.

WALK 20

WESTHOPE COMMON

DESCRIPTION This is a delightful 2 mile moderate walk on Westhope Common and through the remote hamlet of Westhope. There are some excellent views from the top of the Common, more of which can be explored as it is open access land.

START Entrance to Westhope Common, SO 467518. Bus users can do this walk by starting at section 3, having done the first three sections of walk 13 first.

DIRECTIONS From Hereford on the A 4110, turn RIGHT (signed to Westhope) at the end of Canon Pyon village, just after passing the primary school. Turn LEFT at the next junction and then continue until the road ends at a cattle grid. Drive over this to park on the Common.

1 From the cattle grid at the entrance, walk along the left hand edge of the common. When the hedge turns left, keep ahead for about 70 yards. Turn LEFT 90° and walk ahead, crossing a track to reach the boundary. Bear LEFT to walk along a track leading off the common. When it ends, turn LEFT to walk along a grassy track and across a short stretch of common to go through a gate. Turn RIGHT on a road and RIGHT again at the next junction.

2 Take the first fork LEFT off the road on a wide track, opposite a wooden panelled gate on the right. Keep RIGHT at the next junction. Ignore turnings on the left. Pass a house on the right and join its drive to the road. Here, with New House in front of you, turn LEFT. Keep ahead as the road becomes rougher in places until eventually it ends at a house in front of you, Folly Hall Cottage. If completing walk 13, turn RIGHT here down steps and go to Section 4 of walk 13. Otherwise turn LEFT uphill past the cottage to reach a four-way junction. Keep straight ahead.

3 Before long cross a track and continue on a wide grassy stretch. When the route forks into three, take the middle way, to the right of the waymarked byway. Bear LEFT when you reach a track and follow this round to the right and over the cattle grid to the common.

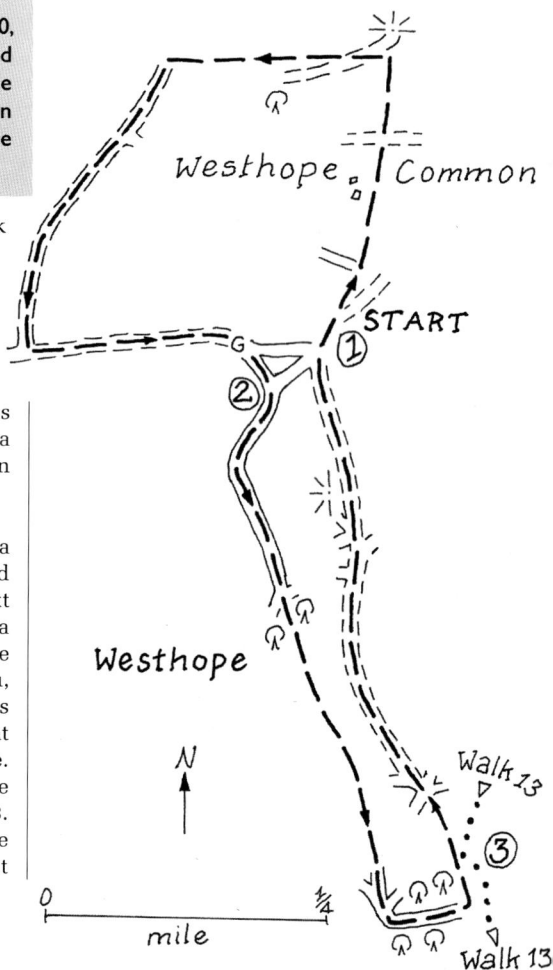

Westhope Common

START

Westhope

N

Walk 13

Walk 13

0   1/4
mile